KEEP KICKING, FRISCO
KEEP KICKING

FRANCISCO M. TORRES, M.D.

Copyright © 2020 by Francisco M. Torres, M.D.
All rights reserved. No part of this publication may be reproduced, distributed, or transmitted in any form or by any means, including photocopying, recording, or other electronic or mechanical methods, without the prior written permission of the publisher, except in the case of brief quotations embodied in critical reviews and certain other noncommercial uses permitted by copyright law.

For bulk orders, permission to quote, or to book the author for a speaking engagement write to the publisher, addressed "Attention: Permissions Coordinator," using one of the methods below.

info@keepkickingfrisco.com

www.keepkickingfrisco.com

Francisco M. Torres

2250 Drew St

Clearwater, Fl. 33765.

727.797.7463

Quantity sales. Special discounts are available on quantity purchases by bookstores, corporations, associations, and others. For details, contact the publisher.

Disclaimer of Warranty of Limit of Liability

The author and publisher make no representations or warranties with respect to the accuracy of the contents of this work and do hereby specifically and expressly disclaim all warranties, including without limitation, warranties of title, merchantability, fitness for a particular purpose and non-infringement. No warranty may be created or extended by sales or promotional material associated with this work.

Any advice, strategies, and ideas contained herein may not be suitable for particular situations. This work is sold with the understanding that the publisher is not engaged in or rendering medical or legal advice or other professional services. If professional assistance is required, the services of a competent professional person should be sought. Consult your health care professionals regarding any symptoms of anxiety, panic disorders, or anything else that requires medical or personal attention.

Although the author and publisher have made every effort to ensure that the information in this book was correct at press time, the author and publisher do not assume and hereby disclaim any responsibility or liability whatsoever to the fullest extent allowed by law to any party for any and all direct, indirect, incidental, special, or consequential damages, or lost profits that result, either directly, or indirectly, from the use and application of any of the contents of this book. The purchaser or reader of this book alone assumes the risk for anything learned from this book.

This book is not intended as a substitute for medical advice and should not be used in such a manner. Furthermore, the use of this book does not establish a doctor-patient relationship.

The information provided is not intended to serve as legal or medical advice. The views expressed herein are solely those of the author and do not reflect the opinions of any other person or entity.

AUTHOR'S NOTE

I have endeavored to tell a true story, but I cannot swear to the accuracy of every detail. I'm a flawed human, and I have to rely on my flawed memories and my subjective experience.

Occasionally, and to respect the privacy of various characters in my life, I have fudged the details on purpose by changing a name here or an identifying characteristic there.

More often, I have done the best I can with the recollections I have. I do not intend that any of these memories be taken as an exact reproduction of what was said or done.

This book is true to my experience, which is to say it's true to me, even if it isn't true to anyone else.

CONTENTS

Author's Note. v
Dedication. xi
Acknowledgments xiii
Foreword xv
Introduction. xxi
Chapter 1: Treading Water 1
Chapter 2: Bittersweet September 7
Chapter 3: Saturnino 16
Chapter 4: Heroes Or Monsters? 22
Chapter 5: On an Island. 29
Chapter 6: Summer Of '69. 39
Chapter 7: Spanish Christmas 45
Chapter 8: Dazed and Confused 50
Chapter 9: Carjacked 53
Chapter 10: Tony Robbins and Pope John Paul Ii. 61
Chapter 11: Panic at 2,000 Feet 68
Chapter 12: Separation Anxiety 76
Chapter 13: Where are You, God? 81
Chapter 14: Back Home. 88
Chapter 15: Therapy 93
Chapter 16: Certain about Uncertainty: Panic for The New Millennium 99
Chapter 17: Earthquake. 107
Chapter 18: Ultra! 116
Chapter 19: The Inca Trail 126
Chapter 20: The Finish Line. 134
Chapter 21: The Train Ride Home. 140
Epilogue: Anxiety in the Time of Coronavirus 148
Afterword. 154
More Books by Francisco M. Torres. 162
About the Author. 164

"Her whole life, my grandma was afraid of lightning. She used to tell me stories of how the English nuns when she was a schoolgirl, would sit her down in front of a large window during a thunderstorm and force her to watch the lightning strikes in hopes that it would cure her. My grandfather, her husband, and a psychiatrist tried to hypnotize her with the same intent. Needless to say, for those of us who knew her, they both failed miserably."

—Jordi I. Torres, Grandson

DEDICATION

I DEDICATE THIS book to my mother, who was indeed afraid of lightning. Sadly, it wasn't the only thing that caused her fear. At a time when seeking mental health treatment was stigmatized, especially in her home country of Spain, she struggled with generalized anxiety.

But my mother didn't live scared. She was courageous, loving, and fierce in her determination to protect her children and her grandchildren from the dangers of this world. Despite her fear of thunderstorms, she moved to Puerto Rico and Florida to be nearest to those she treasured most.

For me, she was the original success story—my role model for how to face my fears and keep trying even when we failed to overcome them. Her legacy lives on in me, my siblings, and all her grandchildren. We love you, Mami.

ACKNOWLEDGMENTS

WRITING A MEMOIR was harder than I thought. But, at the same time, it has been an enriching and humbling experience. I am thankful to those who supported me in the writing of this book.

I am perpetually thankful to my friend and psychotherapist, Mary, who went the extra mile to make certain mine was a successful story despite the odds. Thank you for believing in me and not giving up when occasionally I tried to sabotage my path to recovery. Because of your extraordinary professional care, I have a legacy to pass on to my family where one didn't exist before.

I owe my most enormous debt to my son Jordi for his brilliant editorial suggestions, honest understanding, and encouragement, which made this book imaginable. Thank you also to my brother, Juan Luis, and my sister, Maria, for fact-checking my childhood memories, and supporting my desire to tell what is in part their story too.

My final product benefited greatly from the constructive criticism and scholarly advice of my exceptional writing coach, Clare Levijoki. Many praises to my witty copy editor, Joe Wisinski, as well.

I wish to also acknowledge my valuable research assistants, Katie Roche and April Hollis, for their invaluable work with the scientific aspects of the final manuscript's culmination, including thorough clinical research.

Finally, I have to recognize a remarkable human being. This book would not have been achievable without the encouragement and support, as well as the constructive and occasionally brutal but well-meaning criticisms offered from the very outset by my extraordinary wife, Elvira.

FOREWORD

JORDI I. TORRES

THERE EXISTS A rich literary tradition of stories about inheritance. Several of Shakespeare's most famous plays—like *King Lear* and *The Merchant of Venice*—rely on complicated plots to determine who will inherit what from whom. In *Bleak House,* Charles Dickens catalogues the absurdities of how the legal system adjudicates contested wills, and Jane Austen's *Pride and Prejudice* is famously premised on a father's inability to bequeath his estate to his unmarried daughters. Toni Morrison tackles the trauma of slavery as a type of inheritance in *Beloved*. George Elliot's *Middlemarch* describes how two older men contrive to use their wills as a way to live forever. My dad's memoir is about inheritance too. It's a personal excavation of his own history, but it's also a broader study on how we inherit much more than we realize from our families.

When I was eleven years old, my father asked for my help writing an essay. He was still shy and self-conscious in those days about his English. The essay was important. If it struck the right chord, he could win a cash prize, and more importantly, the top spot on the pages of Men's Health Magazine.

The competition, Body for Life, required participants to demonstrate an astonishing physical transformation over the course of a few months. Thousands of entrants sent dramatic before and after photographs, each candidate gripping a newspaper with the date of publication conspicuously aimed at the camera. My dad knew the essay could make all the difference.

By the time I sat down at his computer, he had already written the first draft. His thesis was clear—the purpose of my transformation is to inspire my oldest son, Jordi, who is overweight. "Can you help make it more powerful?" he asked me.

I edited dutifully under his watchful eye, writing in his voice about my disappointing huskiness. We described all the challenges associated with my weight. We wrote that I was afraid to take my shirt off by the pool and speak up in public. We wrote about the friends I didn't have, the sports I couldn't play, and the future I put in jeopardy because of my addiction to sugar and fried plantains. For our trouble, we received an honorable mention from the magazine, and my dad's impressive before and after photos appeared between the covers. Mercifully, they didn't print his essay.

But some damage to our relationship had been done. The truth is that by sixth grade, I had a large crew of friends at school. I played baseball and football. I was actually pretty outspoken in class, and I dreamed of becoming a television news reporter like my hero, Walter Cronkite. The extra weight would burn off naturally by the end of middle school.

My dad's essay was more about his own experience with anxiety as a heavy pre-teen, but it made me think I had something to be anxious about too. If I wasn't worried over my appearance before ghostwriting the Body for Life entry, I sure was afterward.

For a long time, I approached my father with simmering resentment. He had made me feel uncomfortable in my own skin. Nevertheless, my disdain always mixed uneasily with a desperate need to make my father proud—to prove I wasn't as broken as the essay made me sound. To cope, I convinced myself that my father was selfish and didn't care about me, but only my accomplishments.

As I grew up, I got embarrassed by his eccentricities—professional photoshoots, Gatsbyesque holiday parties, sequined tuxedos. In many ways, I wrote him off. Still, I always strove for his approval.

This book has been a revelation for me, and I think it could be a revelation for others. It is so easy to lose sight of a person when we become blinded by a few of their behaviors, and by our own fraught reactions to them. Every day in my practice as a criminal defense attorney, I watch how the instinct to define others and to judge them with imperfect information plays out in our society. My dad's story is not heroic or tragic. It's human, and it's universal. The beauty is in the details.

I learned a lot about my dad reading his early manuscripts. I read and reread about the tremendous losses of his youth—his precious Aunt Lola, who cared for him when his mother couldn't, his favorite teacher who believed in him when others cast him aside, and even his pet duck who made him feel just a little less alone. Of course, I was old enough to remember when he packed his bags to render aid after Haiti's earthquake and how triumphantly he returned after finishing the Machu Picchu marathon in Peru. But until I read this book, I had no idea how scared he had been to embark on either of those adventures.

My dad's anxieties—the ones we knew about—were a joke to us growing up. When we were younger, my brothers and I would mock how he didn't want to call the restaurant to order pizza if my mom was away. He always made us do it. When he panicked before an amusement park ride, we called him names. If his own father frayed his nerves, we prodded him further just to get a rise.

One day our dad changed. He started attending the Tony Robbins seminars he describes in the book, entering bodybuilding competitions, buying expensive cars, and dressing like an Austin Powers villain. For teenage boys, his newfound confidence was annoying. In hindsight, I know he was searching for a way to break free. He was trying to reinvent himself.

But his acts of reinvention were always stymied by the same shortcoming—a failure to acknowledge and appreciate the genesis of the man he had always been. Only in writing this book has he come to terms with himself. His journey can be a lesson to others.

My dad's memoir is about the things we inherit, but it's also about what we do with what is passed down to us. In explaining his personal history, my dad asks us to be mindful of the long trajectory of our lives, ever-changing and always redeemable. The pages that follow are interesting for their fabulous tales of ultramarathons in the Peruvian Andes and colorful shipwrecks in Hawaii. The reader can expect more than one emotive tale of epic loss, and the occasional almost-mythological twist of fate. However, what makes this book insightful and worth reading is its attention to the little details of life, and its honest examination of the damage we cause each other often without knowing it.

Until the day she died, my grandmother was afraid of lightning. She was anxious about other things too. She lived scared of the coming nuclear wars and serial killers stalking the suburbs. Some of that pathology rubbed off on my dad. He inherited his mother's unease, and he developed his own anxieties. Circumstances conspired to pile on. My grandfather (victim to his own mental health challenges) was cruel towards his young son. My dad lost his early caretaker to cancer. He was carjacked at gunpoint. He began suffering panic attacks.

So how did the man who inherited so much anxiety end up scaling mountains, scuba diving to shipwrecks, and entering body-building competitions? That, too, is a story of inheritance.

My grandmother and her family survived a brutal civil war. Later, she moved away from home to a foreign country, because she thought it was best for her three young children. Her anxiety rubbed off, but so too did her resolve and her striving spirit. Most importantly, she bestowed her unconditional love upon my father, and that inheritance only grows over the course of generations.

My father is also the inheritor of many other kindnesses. His Aunt Lola taught him how to care for others. His Abuelo Ramos bequeathed an entire complex cultural history, and an instinct to thrive under conditions of uncertainty. From his dear friend Paco he absorbed a morality of loyalty, compassion, and hard work. From my mom, he gained an entirely new inheritance of family and self-worth. These were all tools he deployed to accomplish his goals and to overcome his anxiety. None of us does it alone.

I, too, am the beneficiary of my dad's efforts and experiences. The stories in this book belong as much to my brothers and me as they do to him, and I hope one day that they become the patrimony of our children and grandchildren.

Early on in this book, my dad talks about the inheritance of mental health—for worse, but also for better. Traumas are passed down through generations, as is a sense of security. A family history of anxiety is as real as a family history of cancer or diabetes. But the lesson of my dad's life, however, is that we aren't fated to any particular outcome because of our inheritances.

Unlike an economic inheritance, the emotional inheritance we receive from our families is endlessly rich, complicated, and evolving. And family here is broadly defined. Every human being has a family story—many less fortunate than ours. To understand each other, we have to learn to dig deeper, empathize more fully, and draw connections our society is so often ready to discount.

When he started putting together his memoir, my father told me he didn't want to come off as a hero or a saint. He wanted to expose his own failings—the times in his life he had been uncaring, reckless, spiteful, and yes, even selfish. His hope, he said, was to paint the portrait of a real person who, like us, can be both the victim and the perpetrator in any given story.

Despite his failings, my dad is a hero to me. Back when we were writing his Body for Life essay together, he was focused on himself. He was projecting his own insecurities onto me. I know he loved me then, as he always has, but he wasn't thinking about me in those moments. The idea of making a difference in his son's life was a catchphrase, a clever presentation so he could win a prize.

This memoir is the culmination of my dad's Herculean efforts to redefine his life. It may have taken him several months to write, but it took years of self-discovery and reflection. It required coming to terms with how he had sometimes treated others, even those closest to him. In order to recount his life, he had to reopen old wounds and relive more than a few haunting tragedies. I can attest that the transformation my dad describes in this memoir is far more real than any changes manifest in his before or after photos. I am confident that the results will be more lasting too.

My father didn't write this book to win any acclaim. His choice to share his story is a decision to expose the extent to which we can impact those around us inadvertently. Our family is but one example, and anxiety is but one of the human traits we share with our offspring. But by using our story as a springboard, my dad wants his readers to reconsider what we all impart to others by our actions and by our attitudes. It's a challenge to do better and to be more understanding of ourselves and each other.

As far as I am concerned, this book represents my proudest inheritance as the author's son. Thankfully, it's an inheritance we can share with others.

INTRODUCTION

THIS BOOK IS about my lifelong tug of war with anxiety. I am not a celebrity or a politician, and there are no cameos by famous characters in the pages that follow. I have enjoyed great privileges—I was never penniless; I became a doctor; I am a father to four healthy children, and I am married to a supportive wife. I am proud of my achievements—building a successful medical practice from scratch, scuba diving in Tonga, running a marathon through Machu Picchu.

But what I hope makes this story worth reading is the ordinariness of my struggle to overcome fear and confront my insecurities on a path to finding purpose and finally being comfortable in my own skin. The lesson is simple: anxiety can shape you, but it doesn't make you who you are. In the end, we can control it.

My life began in 1960 in Seville, Spain. I started scared. Even as a toddler, I was afraid of death, terrified of change, mortified of the unknown. I grew up bogged down by guilt, fear, and panic.

My parents were not bad people. They, too, were born with a set of psychological challenges and limited world views and beliefs. They, like all of us, sought purpose and a sense of significance. For them, the guiding principle was religion.

At a young age, I left my world behind—my grandparents, my bedroom, my cousins, my neighborhood, my familiar sights, and sounds—and I landed on an island, Puerto Rico. I was thrust into a new family, one where mental disease was the norm. My mother, even more of an outsider than I, was ensnared by its tentacles. It took its toll on her.

My father himself was the victim of an undiagnosed mental illness, which in turn sullied the atmosphere in our family home. The negativity almost tore me down completely. The petty grievances of people defined my purpose in life with a limited worldview.

In school, I lugged around a persistent feeling of sadness and defeat. On the surface, I tried my best to be the boy on the cover of this book—defiant, jovial, and secure. When I closed my eyes, I pictured a different version of myself. I wasn't interested in the good—just the good for me.

I was in my mid-20s the first time I rushed into the emergency room, convinced I was dying. The story would repeat itself, and after a torturous streak of ER visits, I finally diagnosed myself with a panic disorder brought on by severe anxiety.

Wrongheaded, I determined to treat myself without the benefit of therapy or drugs. What followed is the whacky road of self-discovery I describe in this book: the boy with a fear of water who scuba dives into a sunken shipwreck off the coast of Maui, the weak student who becomes a doctor, the anxious doctor who becomes a pilot, the fat kid who starts entering and winning bodybuilding competitions, and the casual runner who signs up for an ultra-marathon in Peru and scales Machu Picchu in a single day.

The accumulated eccentricities of my upbringing are what shaped my accomplishments, my missteps, my anxiety, and my character. They're a monument to resilience, and I hope an inspiration to anyone seeking to understand why they fear and how they can move beyond their fear.

Each of the characters described, more or less accurately, left an indelible mark on my life. In exploring them through this book, I have come to understand better how I became who I am—how I overcame my discomfort. Their stories and mine are meant to be a lesson in the universality of fear, the scourge of anxiety, the dread of panic attacks, but also the resilience of the human mind and spirit.

My basic thesis is that much of our anxiety ultimately derives from shame, guilt, and narcissism—most of it inculcated in us before we even have a fighting chance. But life is the fight, and by delving into our history, we can build our future selves—happy, healthy, and ready to cope with our anxiety.

This book consists mostly of stories from my life—many of which I've been told are bizarre and extraordinary enough to be gripping and entertaining. But I'll also include brief discussions of scientific findings providing the answers to questions about where anxiety comes from, what daily choices can help us take control of our lives, and exactly how much these choices can help us.

Perceptions change our reality, and those perceptions color our opinions and attitudes about mental health. I sincerely hope that this book might change your perceptions about anxiety and panic disorders.

By many measures, my life has been a resounding success. But this book shows that success is relative, and paths to success are varied, especially for those of us who bear the added burden of mental illness.

I want to prove that you don't have to change anything about yourself to overcome anxiety. Instead, I want to model how you can strengthen yourself by better understanding the gaps that sometimes make it hard for us to reach our full potential. I want you to learn from my mistakes and recognize tools that might help you in your journey.

Our brains are the masters of our reality. Facts don't make you miserable—it's your perception of the facts. If we are fortunate to exercise even a little control, we need to take care of our minds and become intentional about how we experience and react to the world.

If our brains are enveloped in darkness, we can't ever really see the sunshine. As I learned the hard way, this requires keeping an open mind and a positive attitude. It means setting aside jealousies and grudges. It means training our brains, with the help of psychotherapy and other treatments if necessary, but always with one goal in mind—to be at peace and to become our best selves.

Life only gives us one chance to live out our destiny. No matter how much you're struggling right now, your future is to enjoy the world for all its marvels and leave your beautiful mark on its surface.

CHAPTER 1

TREADING WATER

I DID NOT belong at the controls of an airplane. When I drive my car, I ride the brakes, and I get anxious about changing lanes in traffic. As the plane took flight, I felt my chest muscles tighten. I started panting, not breathing. The instructor had tricked me. He had jumped out of the plane as it started. There I was, climbing into the clouds, alone.

Getting a pilot's license requires a successful solo flight, but I could have flown with my instructor forever. I didn't need the license. I was in my comfort zone, knowing the instructor was there to save me. My instructor was at his wit's end. His desperation had driven him to the ruse.

I clung to the control wheel. My lungs filled with what felt like water. I was drowning, and it was a familiar sensation.

Before my 5th birthday, while I was still living in Spain, I nearly drowned in the sea of San Lucas de Barrameda, near Cadiz. It was supposed to be a pleasant family outing to the beach. I had wandered out to the water. I was happy.

My next memory is of a ferocious white wave sucking me deep into the seabed. I bounced out past the shallows, desperate for air. I swallowed saltwater, and I waved frantically at my family.

My mother shrieked in panic from shore, and my older brother, Juan Luis, bounded into the surf to save me. Dragged back onshore by Juan Luis, I listened, a little disoriented, to my mother and my brother, exhaling their terror at the situation. I could have died, they said. I was almost gone. They described their helplessness, and for the first time in my young life, I consciously feared death. Juan Luis was only seven years old then.

I almost mythologized drowning after that. It was a boogeyman who haunted my dreams. Water became associated with death. This proved especially challenging for me when, at the age of six, we moved to Puerto Rico to be with my father's family.

Water is everywhere in Puerto Rico. Not only is the Caribbean never more than a couple of hours away, but there are also pools everywhere too. I didn't want to learn to swim. The prospect was hair-raising. So, when my mother coolly informed me that I would be enrolled in swim lessons, I wanted to hide in the closet under the stairs and never come out. I visualized swallowing buckets of chlorinated water and sinking lifelessly to the bottom of the pool.

The thing about anxieties and phobias is that they are rarely cabined to one instigating stimulus or circumstance. I was fearful of many things, even as a pre-teen boy. Unfortunately for me, swim lessons at the local pool implicated another one of my greatest fears.

I was husky. There's no denying it. But I felt absolutely disgusting. I became fixated at the size of my breasts. I thought they were too large for a boy. On more than one occasion, it crossed my mind that others were staring at my chest. I was worried someone might mistake me for a girl.

Once, back in Spain, my grandmother, Abuela Candida, ordered me out of the apartment so she and her sister could clean it, as they did every morning. My mom was visiting friends with my brother and sister. I wasn't thrilled about going out by myself, but I felt the pressure to leave, so I mustered the courage to quiet my fears and to walk down to the hectic streets of downtown Seville.

I chose the route I was used to walking with my grandfather,

Abuelo Ramos. I wandered for a while and turned onto a busy street crowded with fast-moving automobiles and frenzied pedestrians on their way to work. Suddenly, I felt a vigorous squeeze of my left arm. It took me by surprise. The fingers around my bicep were tight and ferocious. And then the older man's face came into view. A pair of oversize Buddy Holly glasses magnified his buggy eyes, eclipsing even his enormous nose. I swiveled my head, desperate for someone to notice, but the crowds continued on about their business.

The first thing that came into my mind was the thought this aged man had confused me for a girl. I was wearing a tight polo shirt, which made me self-conscious of my chest. In my mind, he couldn't possibly have intended to snatch a boy.

I fought against the older man's grip, and he let me go after a little fight. I was so scared I don't remember how I got back to the apartment. I didn't tell anyone. The encounter was terrifying enough on its own, but it also reinforced my negative feelings about my body. One can imagine how debilitating the notion of drowning shirtless at a swim lesson was for me.

But my mom insisted. She said it would be fun. It was not.

The day was hot, even for the summer in San Juan. There were ten students in the class, including my brother and me. Many of the parents mingled by the side of the pool, looking at their children. Our parents had driven off in my father's new '68 green Falcon—a day off from me, I thought.

My brother already knew how to swim. Some other kids did too. I kept my t-shirt on as long as I could, hoping for an intervening mercy to prevent me from fully baring my anxieties. The comfort of being fully clothed didn't last long. Everyone had to get ready to swim, and I pulled my t-shirt off nervously.

The instructor welcomed us. His arms were massive and shapely. I stared at the little veins bulging out from under his tight skin. He was bald as a cue ball, but he was confident and didn't speak Spanish. At the time, I hated speaking English. I had trouble pronouncing it, and I was always nervous that I had said the wrong word.

Mr. Winston was from California, and he had been in the Army. His teeth shimmered in the sunshine as he asked us to introduce ourselves. "Loud and clear! Like you're proud of it," he said. When my turn came, I screamed at the top of my lungs, "Francisco!" My voice cracked, and it felt like all the other kids were snickering.

Mr. Winston was impressed. "All right, Frisco! Just like back home—San Francisco. I like your style."

Right then, Mr. Winston's partner emerged from inside. She was almost as tall as Mr. Winston, and she had a kind of blonde hair I had only ever seen on television. Her name was Ms. Giovanini.

"What's all the excitement out here?" she asked playfully.

She was beautiful. I couldn't stop staring. But then I remembered I was topless. I twisted and turned to hide my exposed torso. I moved my arms out in front of my chest and sucked in my stomach. My cheeks felt warm. I looked down at my toes.

"We've got a Frisco over here," Mr. Winston said, drawing the beautiful blonde's attention to me. I despised him. I hated the nickname Frisco. That wasn't my nickname. My nickname was Kiko, and only my family and close friends were allowed to call me Kiko. I tried to smile in front of the woman. Even I didn't believe my smile was sincere.

The two instructors gave a brief above-water tutorial about how to remain afloat. Then, within minutes, it was time to line up at the deep end of the pool. The woman was already in the water, waiting for us. There were no life vests or flotation devices of any kind. I was sixth in line, trying not to pee my pants, contorting desperately to hide my chubbiness from Ms. Giovanini.

At Mr. Winston's command, Mario—a classmate who would later become my best friend—jumped into the water. How did he end up going first? He was the only one who looked almost as scared as I did. The splash was tentative, but then he began thrashing.

Poor Mario flailed about as the other students laughed riotously from dry land. I was searching for him in the water until Mr. Winston reached his tree-trunk arm in and plucked Mario out.

"Good try, little guy," he said as poor Mario heaved air and water out onto the deck. "Next!" Mr. Winston commanded.

The other students fared better than Mario. They floated with varying success, making it in time to the other side of the pool. My turn came eventually.

"Let's go, man. Let's go," Mr. Winston shouted as if he was ordering me to parachute out of a plane and onto the battlefield. I ran up, stopped short, but as soon as I could feel Mr. Winston reaching toward me, I decided I had better choose my own fate. I leaped into the water.

At first I sank, paralyzed by fear and the surprise of the water against my eyes and mouth. I flashed back to the dark ocean off the coast of Spain, my mother shrieking on the shore. I panicked. I breathed in a little water, convinced this was the end for me. I closed my eyes, so my ears popped. Somehow, I paddled up to the surface, further up than Mario had. I saw Ms. Giovanini, her arms stretched out, beckoning me.

Then I heard it: "Keep kicking, Frisco. Keep kicking." Mr. Winston was coaching me from the deck. His girlfriend was smiling and egging me on too.

"Keep kicking, Frisco," I said to myself.

It would not be the last time I would resort to this mantra. Those of us who have lived with acute anxiety and panic are familiar with the onrush of fear—a fear of dying. Fear is a natural human instinct. An essential psychological feature for survival. Anxiety disorders co-opt this architecture and deploy fear irrationally to build up phobias and unnatural terror.

Throughout my life I would come to treat critically ill patients, scuba dive in Fiji and Tonga, immigrate to a new country, enter and win a bodybuilding competition, run an ultra-marathon in the mountains of Peru, and yes, even take the reins of a Cessna. That isn't because the anxiety and fear magically went away. I am, and have always been, a version of the boy scared of drowning shirtless in front of that beautiful blonde instructor.

But Mr. Winston's words have been a persistent echo of motivation. That pool was the starting gate for my life-long race to live a full life. I started to learn the real lesson of Mr. Winston's class—Keep Kicking.

And I was kicking so hard I almost didn't notice when a pair of angelic hands rescued me from certain death. I saw Ms. Giovanini, her arms stretched out toward me. She pulled me in close, and I was in heaven. I felt loved, safe, and cared for. The initial feeling of abandonment, lingering from when my mother dropped us off, had vanished.

All the parents, watching by the poolside, cheered and giggled. They, too, were afraid I would drown. My parents were nowhere to be found.

Like everything in life, this story is a mixed bag.

CHAPTER 2

BITTERSWEET SEPTEMBER

I WAS BORN in Seville, Spain. We lived under the dictatorship of Generalissimo Francisco Franco, whose strict religiosity and anti-socialism infected every aspect of daily life. I am ashamed to admit that my parents might have named me in his honor. Or maybe it really was after my godfather, as they once told me.

The moment that my mother had been expecting, or maybe dreading, for the last nine months had arrived. I was born at a local clinic, brought to life by the family obstetrician, Dr. Aznar, who had delivered my brother two years prior. I am told that my father was physically present.

It was a mid-afternoon birth—*siesta* time in Spain when most people would be home resting or taking a nap. It probably had an impact on who was in the delivery room. Winston Churchill first popularized the custom of an afternoon nap in the English-speaking world. He had learned during joint operations with Spanish forces that a midday nap could allow him and his men to work into the late hours of the night with fresh minds and energy.

My delivery into this world was not an easy one, the story goes, and at the end, I exhausted my mother from arduous pushing and screaming. They removed me almost immediately from her arms to the nursery.

One day when I was four years old, while my mother was struggling to get my head through the opening of a turtleneck shirt, I relived the trauma of being born. My mother pulled the tight fabric down over my crown and behind my ears. The tightness was painful as the shirt squeezed my head. I winced, and my father joked about how big my head was. He reminded me of how I had hurt my mother.

"It was like pushing a watermelon through a hole the size of a lemon," my father said. "She must have felt like she was being ripped in half."

My mother added, "I lost my voice screaming. It was the worst pain of my life."

This wouldn't be the last time my dad referred this way to my birth or my enormous head.

After my birth, my mother struggled with undiagnosed postpartum depression. My great aunt told me that after I was born, my mother's behavior changed. She became sad, quiet, and withdrawn. My aunt recalled her as perennially tired and uninterested in going out. She continued to smoke during the pregnancy, and once I was born the habit grew even more important for her.

From a very young age, my family joined my father in ridiculing me about how large my head was at birth, and how I had destroyed my mother's insides. My father made sure I would remember for the rest of my life how much pain I had caused her.

Believe it or not, my father was actually a practicing psychiatrist. Growing up, I did not make much of that fact. As I aged, it was hard not to wonder whether he recognized the psychological consequences of his behavior toward us. I believe he did it to inflict pain. His penchant for psychological abuse grew more vicious the older he got.

In those days, we saw doctors as gods. They were untouchable. You were told never to question them and to follow their orders. They were honest and opinionated. Those same doctors, however, tended not to be very empathetic. They didn't train for good bedside manners.

My father, as a psychiatrist, used every weapon he had learned from his extensive medical studies against his psychological opponents, including his family. Even though on the outside he was a very religious and affectionate man he knew how to inflict pain with his words.

In church every Sunday he would meet with the priest for confession before Mass. A few moments after he left the confessional, he would come back to the pew where we were sitting. He would push me to the side to let him in, and he could never spare a kind word. He looked angry and uncomfortable with me by his side.

My father was a master, like a chameleon, at changing his appearance in front of certain people. He was always trying to analyze our behavior and to simplify our responses to different situations in order to disarm us.

However, he never believed in treatment for himself, even though my mom told us that at one point he required medication because he was hearing voices and becoming paranoid about his coworkers.

My mother related that on more than one occasion, her cousin Jaime had to escort my father back to the university because my father believed he was receiving messages through telepathy telling him it was dangerous to attend. He claimed that his thoughts were being intercepted by radio broadcasting devices implanted in his brain.

Religious images obsessed him, particularly of the Holy Virgin Mary. He was a devoted worshiper of the Virgin of Lourdes, and he always carried with him a small plastic statuette, full of holy water from Lourdes in France. Paradoxically, he also believed strongly in astrology and the zodiac signs.

My father had an aversion to planning for the future, to planning and organizing to achieve a worthy goal, to enjoying his profession, and to buying a house. My Spanish grandmother, Candida, thought of him as a "lazy island man."

Today, with all my medical education and my passion for psychology, I believe that he was a functional paranoid, narcissistic schizophrenic, suffering a milder version of many of the same symptoms as his diagnosed schizophrenic mother. He could cope with the delusions and paranoia and manage the everyday functioning of his life, but they were a persistent source of torment for him and for us.

As a boy in Spain, I used to play with a neighbor who was my same age. Manolito was thinner and more agile than me, and he appeared to be more confident and independent. He was more curious and adventurous than I could ever hope to become. His parents always dressed him in fine white shorts, with his chestnut hair meticulously combed to the side. His mother was a good family friend of ours, and we used to meet at church on Sundays and walk back to the house where we spent a few hours together.

One day, I told my aunt I wasn't feeling well. They called the doctor who, after examining me, diagnosed a straightforward case of the mumps. My brother got them too.

I don't remember the disease itself. The pain was inflicted after I had recovered. My father appeared in my bedroom. He never came into my bedroom. Maybe he was happy I had survived, I thought. Perhaps he realized how sorry he would be if I had not come through. He came over to my bed, and he put his hand on my forehead.

"You know that you passed along your disease to your friend, Manolito?" he asked me.

I nodded sheepishly, crestfallen.

"Well," my father added, "your friend didn't survive. He died."

This wasn't the last I heard of my connection to my friend's death. Later on my father would connect me to his passing, and he used the incident against me, even if it was in cruel jest. The list of incidents I felt guilty about was growing. More and more, I thought I couldn't control when and how I hurt others—my mom, my friend.

Later on, my father's psychological bullying would emigrate with me across the Atlantic Ocean to his birthplace.

There is an unofficial holiday celebrated each year on Sept. 23, known as *El Grito de Lares*. It commemorates the failed insurrection against the ruling Spanish government in 1868. Lares is a mountain town in the western region of Puerto Rico, nestled on a ridge over 3,900 feet above sea level. Sept. 23 is my birthday.

My father used the word *grito* (scream) as an analogy to my mother's screams the day I was born. He told and retold me how her screaming was so intense because of the terrible pain caused by the size of my head. He was not shy about sharing this with whoever was present that day at the house to celebrate my birthday.

Once the house was teeming with family and friends, he would stand up and say: "In our house, we call this day 'The Scream of Manoli' in remembrance of how she screamed while delivering Kiko and his colossal head."

Everybody always laughed. They were laughing at me and my big head. More than once, he repeated this story to me even before wishing me a happy birthday. I started to hate my birthday.

My mother wasn't mentally or physically prepared to care for me after my birth. She became attentive only to my brother's needs. She felt incapable of taking care of two children. I don't remember any close interaction with her during those early years of my life. For this reason, my parents delivered me to the attention of my great aunt on my grandmother's side, Tia Lola, who lived with us at my grandparents' home.

Tia Lola became my protector. I accompanied her to the market every morning and she was always interceding on my behalf in front of my parents or strangers. I felt loved and safe. One day, and with no warning, I noticed that she was not in her usual bedroom anymore. They placed her in another room at the far end of the apartment. She never left the room, and I was not allowed to visit.

Abuela Candida came to me and said, "Your Tia Lola is not feeling well. She needs rest, so you can't be with her. Besides, what she has may be contagious, and I know you don't want to get sick." That day they assigned me to my other great aunt, Tia Pilar, who also lived with us in the apartment.

Tia Pilar was my brother's godmother, which supposed a sacred responsibility for her. Her duty was to take care of him in case my parents became unable. This was a doctrine taught by the Catholic Church. She was a very religious woman, devoted to her faith, and she viewed this duty as having been assigned by God. This role gave purpose and meaning to her life. In turn, I felt like an additional burden for Tia Pilar—though she did her best to care for me.

Tia Pilar never married or dated, and my grandparents provided her with food and shelter for taking care of the house and all its needs. Being her older sister, la Abuela Candida controlled all her activities and gave her an allowance in return for loyalty and servitude.

She was a kind woman who accepted me with no complaints, even though her heart belonged to my brother. She was loving and gentle while taking care of all my basic needs. However, I never felt again the deep love that my Tia Lola had for me.

In those days, Spain was superstitious, provincial, and a little backward. Cancer carried a deep stigma because of its association with death. This attitude interfered with everyone's willingness to discuss the condition with others outside the family circle. The diagnosis was not even shared with the patient. The doctors didn't think it would help. They saw cancer as a shameful disease.

For a time, even medical professionals feared that cancer could be contagious and that it would always be fatal. People were uncomfortable talking about the disease and preferred to ignore it—even the doctors.

At the time of Tia Lola's death, I was just four years old. Years later, I learned that Tia Lola died from breast cancer. My family never told me that Tia Lola was suffering from a terminal illness. They hid the truth from me, so I could never prepare for her leaving. I resented this for a long time.

The sudden disappearance of my primary caretaker and the emotional unavailability of my mother resulted in a deep-rooted fear of abandonment that has accompanied me throughout my entire life.

And this was likely not the only contributor to my high levels of childhood anxiety. My mother also had anxiety and trauma, which probably helped increase my anxiety both through her epigenetics and her behavior as a parent.

Research has confirmed that happenings in the womb and during infancy can have a profound impact on a child's sense of well-being, through the mechanism of epigenetics. The results can last for decades, and can even persist into subsequent generations.

In laboratory experiments, science has shown that mice who are stressed during infancy have offspring with heightened anxiety responses and a higher risk of depression. This is true even when their offspring are raised under healthy, safe conditions.

When mice experience stress like that which is created by mortal danger in infancy, nature turns up their default fear and anxiety responses to help keep them safe. Nature even makes sure that this heightened awareness of potential danger is passed on to their offspring, also if their offspring don't experience such stress themselves.[1]

My mother suffered as a young child from a severe phobia to thunderstorms. It is not possible to pinpoint for sure the origin of this condition, but it is hard not to see a connection to my mother's exposure at a very young age to the bombing of her hometown during the Spanish Civil War.

Some phobias persist as habits long after the emotional conflict or trauma which gave origin to them have disappeared. Many fears dissolve away as you grow up, but many don't.

My mother told us that during her school years, she had often been in a state of considerable tension. She feared that her school friends and teachers would ridicule her if she felt the need to seek refuge from thunder by hiding in a closet or a restroom. She recalled a warm day at school when the skies darkened to a bluish-gray. She predicted an impending storm.

In the distance, she could hear a soft but growing rumble of thunder. The wind picked up, slashing at the classroom windows, and the thunder roared far away. My mother trembled, her palms sweaty. She succumbed to heavy and uncontrollable panting. She

---

1   Franklin, T. B., Russig, H., Weiss, I. C., Graff, J., Linder, N., Michalon, A.,… Mansuy, I. M. (2010). Epigenetic Transmission of the Impact of Early Stress Across Generations. *Biological Psychiatry, 68*(5), 408–415. Retrieved from https://www.biologicalpsychiatryjournal.com/article/S0006-3223(10)00576-7/fulltext

looked for a place to hide. She asked one of her best friends, Cristina, to accompany her into a supply closet.

"Please, Cristina," she said to her, "stay with me until the storm passes. I am begging you. I promise to help you with your homework or whatever you want! I swear."

Cristina agreed to stay with her even though they were in the middle of class. She knew that both of them risked punishment for skipping school from the authoritarian nuns who ran the school.

Once the storm had passed and my mother felt relief from her anxiety, Cristina and my mother returned to class and were confronted by Sor Teresa, who had been looking for them all over the school premises.

Sor Teresa admonished them. She sentenced them to stay in the chapel and confess with Father Leopoldo. They were banned from lunch for five days, and Sor Teresa promised to report the infraction to their parents.

My mother once told me that in the beginning, after this episode at school, her English nuns tried to control her symptoms by introducing her to the worst thunderstorms as they were happening—leaving her exposed in front of a large window. They literally locked her outside with the storm.

I believe that what the nuns did was well-intentioned. According to their thinking, facing your fears was how you overcame them. Panic disorder as a clinical diagnosis was not included in the DSM III of psychiatry until the late 1980s. The condition was not recognized as treatable. It was not recognized at all.

Today, we know that exposure therapy or flooding can be useful under close medical supervision. In their defense, the English nuns were early, intuitive proponents of the method. However, they did not approach this in a gradual, gentle way. Their unwitting experiment failed and my mother's condition worsened.

As an adult, my mother's phobia of thunderstorms became worse. Her anxieties and fears escalated. My father, out of frustration, tried to hypnotize her, hoping it would cure her. He didn't have any luck.

Every afternoon, like clockwork, while living in Florida, which has regular, violent, summer lightning storms, my mom would retreat to her safe place in one of the house's walk-in closets.

Her entire day revolved around the sky and the weather report. I don't remember when she started using prescribed Serax, an addictive benzodiazepine used for anxiety and insomnia, but it became an intrinsic part of our lives. Without realizing it, she became dependent on these little pills, and many times she asked for them on a sunny day or under a clear evening sky.

Her agony and sadness became evident in her facial expression until the day she died. In some ways, my anxiety was inherited and in other ways, it was imposed.

CHAPTER 3

SATURNINO

THE FIRST CLEAR memory I have is watching President John F. Kennedy's funeral with my family on a large black-and-white TV screen when I was three years old. I am certain I didn't quite understand the reason for the uproar then, but I had no trouble discerning the gloominess plastered on the faces in the room.

I felt inexplicably terrified and sad over the death of this man whom I didn't know, a man who lived and died an ocean away. Both my grandmother and my Tia Pilar were sobbing hysterically.

Abuela said to my aunt through tears, "I can't believe they've killed him. He's a saint! A martyr!"

My aunt replied that it was a punishment for the paganism and sin running rampant in America.

My father exclaimed, "It was the CIA!"

John F. Kennedy was the first American Catholic to occupy the Oval Office. This alone forged a sturdy bond between Spain, the self-perceived Mecca of Catholicism, and the United States. It was my first connection with America.

From that point forward, I grew up scared, carrying the same sense of trepidation with me wherever I went. My parents raised us strictly, adhering to even the most archaic tenants of our Spanish-Catholic faith. At that early age, I was afraid of dying and uncomfortable at any hint of change or uncertainty. The idea of hell petrified me.

They had fought The Spanish Civil War along religious lines. The Republican government targeted the Catholic clergy with such ruthlessness that the carnage is often compared to the Russian Civil War of 1917—the communist revolution. Some estimates conclude that over 7,000 clergy members were executed in the massacre.

Not 30 days after the outbreak of war, Church leaders spoke out in favor of General Francisco Franco's military movement, tying the Church's future to the fate of the coup—for better and for worse.

The conflict made its way into our home. My grandmother always told us the story of her brother Eladio and how the Republican soldiers had imprisoned him, ostensibly for defending his Christian faith.

Abuelo Eladio, as I knew him, was marched every day of his incarceration to a large open grave, handcuffed to another prisoner. The guards would position the two of them at the brim of the large hole, and without warning, they would shoot one from behind.

The choice of who got killed seemed arbitrary. Both men would fall into the grave, and after some time the guards would retrieve the survivor and march him back to his cell. The next day, they repeated the drill.

Franco's military forces liberated Abuelo Eladio, but he had to be confined to a mental institution for the rest of his life. The torture had splintered his psyche.

Franco and his fascist government took full control of Spain in 1939. His regime would be forever aligned with Spain's Catholic Church. Catholicism became the state religion—a departure from the Second Spanish Republic which had existed previously since 1931. Under the protection and promotion of the government, the Church took on a central role in education, health care, and other aspects of civic life. The crucifix featured prominently in government offices and classrooms.

The regime appointed bishops and subsidized salaries for priests. Catholic religious instruction was mandatory for citizens, and the laws of the State reflected the dogma of the Church—banning abortion, abolishing divorce, and criminalizing the sale of contraceptives.

Spain, in the 1960s, was recovering from the devastation of Franco's brutal civil war. Up to 200,000 people had died of starvation during the early years of Francoism, a period known as *Los Años de Hambre* (the Years of Hunger). After a decade of widespread famine and poor financial decisions, Spain was making economic progress.

Fortunately, we were doing better than many of those who were struggling.

Several months after my Tia Lola passed away, when I was still four years old, my grandmother bought me a baby duck. I thought she had given me this cute little ducky as my pet and companion, a consolation for losing my aunt. Abuela Candida had other plans.

We lived on the top floor of our apartment building, and we had direct access to the flat roof above us, which had a rudimentary kitchen and a small bathroom. Abuela Candida and her other sister, Tia Pilar, used this area to raise chickens and rabbits.

The animals were not raised as pets. My great-aunt, Tia Pilar, and Abuela Candida raised them for slaughter—a slaughter executed by their own hands. I remember seeing headless chickens hanging upside down from the drying rack to collect their blood underneath in a pan. The women would bake the blood and serve it for dinner.

My duck arrived at our home with his mother and several siblings. I remember the joy. The sadness I had from the recent loss of my Tia Lola vanished. I was happy and hopeful.

I named my baby duck Saturnino. He had a beautiful silvery-white chest with colored feathers. His head was shiny green with a large beak. Saturnino and I grew close. He used to follow me wherever I went, as long as I had a few grains in my palm.

We had a small kid's plastic pool where he used to splash water with his large webbed feet. At night he stayed on the top floor with his other siblings. I always wanted to bring him down to sleep with me.

After a few months, the unthinkable happened. One night, after having a delicious dinner and feeling full, I went upstairs to check on Saturnino.

I looked for him everywhere. "Saturnino, where are you?" I wanted to kiss my friend goodnight. After calling him several times to no avail, I went running downstairs and asked my grandmother if she had seen him.

"Abuela," I said with panic in my voice, "have you seen Saturnino?"

The look on her face said it all. She stared at the dinner table and pointed to the tall aluminum pot. She answered matter-of-factly, "You just ate that duck for dinner."

The entire world crashed at my feet. Months earlier, my entire family had wailed in front of a television set over a foreign politician none of us had ever met. I had found myself saddened by President Kennedy's assassination. And now, my grandmother, ever so coolly, reported the murder of my precious pet without batting an eye.

I got sick to my stomach, and I wanted to vomit. I went to my bedroom and cried for the entire night. I felt betrayed and unloved. My mind went right to Tia Lola, who had been taken from me, hidden in her bedroom to die out of sight. The accumulation of loss overwhelmed me. I sensed I was being slowly abandoned.

At a young age, I became inconsolably anxious, in part because of my mother's insecure and ambivalent attachment to me. My mother moved about the world as if she were expecting her next misfortune, alert for every danger or uncertainty. She didn't have the mental or emotional reserve she needed to project love and safety onto me.

Still, I clung to my mother, becoming very agitated in response to the remotest possibility of separation. She was self-absorbed and distant, anxious, and distracted by her preoccupations, but I always feared her disapproval of my behavior. I couldn't stand the idea of being rejected. The foundations for my future panic and anxiety had been laid.

And I am not alone among people with anxiety disorders. Early childhood trauma, and even trauma passed down through generations, has been demonstrated to make long-lasting genetic changes in humans as well as laboratory animals. Genes specifically linked to anxiety, depression, and metabolic health are affected.

In 2016, Rachel Yehuda of Mount Sinai Hospital and her colleagues found that Holocaust survivors and their children both had evidence of abnormal methylation in a region of a gene associated with stress. This finding suggests that the survivor's trauma was passed onto their offspring through DNA.[2]

Some people have inherited stress. They may have stress-related symptoms despite not having experienced stressful life events themselves.

Researchers believe that not all children of trauma may manifest these effects under normal conditions. But when we experience severe or chronic stress, our early childhood experiences and even our parents' and grandparents' experiences may influence how we react and our chances of developing severe anxiety, depression, and other mental illnesses.

Scientific research removes bias and allows us to be sure of the effects we see in the world. But it is often artists and philosophers who teach us how to use the knowledge we find. In a 2019 article, writer Brianna Wiest reminds us that "pivot characters" — people who radically change their own lives, breaking familial patterns—can transform the lives of entire generations of their families.

"In the same way that we inherit certain traits, preferences, and characteristics," Wiest tells us, "we also receive memories, traumas, imprints, and patterns, many of which have a profound impact not only on the course of our own lives but also on those generations to come."[3]

In 2013, Professor Marcus Pembrey from University College in

---

[2] Yehuda, R., & Lehrner, A. (2018). Intergenerational transmission of trauma effects: putative role of epigenetic mechanisms. *World Psychiatry, 17*(3), 243–257. doi: 10.1002/wps.20568

[3] Wiest, B. (2019, December 5). Your Family's Behavioral Patterns Are In Your DNA. Retrieved from https://humanparts.medium.com/the-old-emotional-experiences-of-your-ancestors-might-be-running-your-life-today-ac9ec5233c80

London told the BBC that there is no doubt that personal experiences can affect the mental health of subsequent generations.

Specifically, he described how these generational inheritances can be "relevant to phobias, anxiety, and post-traumatic stress disorders" providing compelling evidence that these problems might be better attributed to nature than nurture, or at least to a more lively combination.[4]

Even the best parenting might not be enough to erase the effects of past generations of familial trauma or stress. And anxiety and depression are not personal failures—they are survival responses that have been learned by our family line.

For me, my familial dysfunction seeded my own anxiety. It isn't fair to put that blame entirely on my mother or my grandmother. They were subject to the same influences I was. But I wish I had known what effect these childhood experiences were unwittingly imposing on me. In hindsight, I understand how important our family history can be to our psychological profile. Part of overcoming my anxiety has been understanding its deepest roots.

---

4   Gallagher, J. (n.d.). 'Memories' pass between generations. *BBC News Health*. Retrieved from https://www.bbc.com/news/health-25156510

CHAPTER 4

HEROES OR MONSTERS?

MANUELA RAMOS BORREGO, my mother, was born in 1934 in Spain at the beginning of a violent political conflict, which would soon escalate into a horrific civil war. She grew up in a small town, Villanueva de Ríos y Minas, a few miles north of Seville, the capital of Andalucía.

In the 16th century, Villanueva del Rio was a small outpost within the Kingdom of Seville, in the Sierra de Constantina mountain range, on the banks of the River Guadalquivir. In the 17th century, they discovered new coal mines near the center of town, and King Felipe III allowed the mineral coal to be transported in barges along the Guadalquivir and into Seville.

They established a small suburb next to the principal town to support the new industry, Villanueva de las Minas. The mines of Villanueva became so successful and led to so much wealth that the neighborhood grew into the civic center of the region. The mines operated until 1972, at the end of the Franco regime.

Two years after my mother was born, her town was one of only a handful that suffered over 200 documented murders. Many more went undocumented, as did a torrent of war crimes against women and those the nascent regime deemed to be undesirable. Many young women between the ages of 16 and 22 were kidnapped, tortured, raped, or killed. The Spanish Republic was coming apart at the seams, revealing a sordid underbelly of hatred and sadism.

When my mother was just two years old, the Republican Army suffered a bloody defeat at the Battle of the Ebro. The war exposed my mother, then a toddler, to exploding munitions, the sound of gunshots, and civil unrest characterized by chaos and uncertainty. There was fear in the air and violence on the streets.

Perhaps most of all, it exposed her to the terror and anxiety of those around her—the adults who feared for their lives and the lives of their children when they heard explosions and gunshots. This could easily teach a young child that mortal terror was the proper response to life.

My grandfather, Abuelo Ramos, was serving in the police department in 1937 during the waning days of the Republic. A jealous co-worker accused him of loyalties to the rebel Nationals and General Franco. My grandfather had served with Franco in the army, and his enemies used this against him. They jailed my grandfather for six months, where he spent most of the civil war.

His absence destroyed my mother and my grandmother, Abuela Candida. They were helpless, caught alone amid the flying bullets. They lost their primary source of income.

When Franco's forces declared victory in March 1939, my family's fortunes changed. The conquering Nationals declared my grandfather a hero because they believed he had spent months in jail defending them. In reality, he had never taken sides in the conflict at all, but he was smart enough to keep his mouth shut.

These were times when men and women disloyal to the new regime were executed in the streets. It was a war, but even for war, it was fierce. As we've read in history books and seen in recent times, civil wars bring out the worst in people.

After the Nationals liberated him from jail, Abuelo Ramos got a new job at the police department, coming to lead it. My Abuela Candida received a government pension till the day she died.

My grandparents' marriage was an exemplar for the ideal chauvinistic relationship in a society masking deep matriarchal power—the man wielded outward control. At the same time, the woman made clandestine decisions in the home.

My mother grew up fearing her mother and worshiping her father. Amid chaos and uncertainty, her father was shelter and stability. My mother would continue to mourn him decades after his death. She never recovered from his loss.

My grandfather's legacy is complicated—both within the family and regarding the broader regime.

Every Christmas, our house was packed full of gifts from scores of people who felt they owed my grandfather a favor. They came with cheeses, ham, chickens, and home-made casseroles. I learned later in life that the "favors" they owed my grandfather were often their lives or the lives of close family members.

Throughout this period of Spanish history, the regime inflicted great pain on political dissenters, common criminals, vagrants, homosexuals, and the disabled. Many of those deemed objectionable by the regime were subjected to a gruesome murder by the *garrote vil*—a medieval execution tool, legal in Spain from 1820 until 1978 for capital punishment.

My grandfather used his position in the police department to generate favorable reports and spare dozens of innocents from this terrible fate. Of course, this means he also took no action to save others. He was probably responsible for many senseless executions.

Like many people living in Spain during this dark period of the country's history, the circumstances forced my grandfather to make stark choices and to take sides in a conflict he never advocated or wanted. Without a doubt, he didn't always make the right choice or choose the right side. He lost contact with his family in Catalonia, who disowned him for his participation in the regime they hated. Franco was cruel and genocidal toward Catalonia in particular, where my grandfather was from. This story of family strife was not unique to mine in Franco's Spain. It was the norm.

Abuelo Ramos, for me, was a pillar of strength and security. Whenever I was with him, I felt protected. Only with him, all my fears disappeared and I felt grounded. I wanted to be like him—big and tall (he was 6 foot, 5 inches), practical, brave, and confident. I recall our long daily morning walks after breakfast.

Despite my feeling of proximity to him, I now realize that we saw the world very differently. Abuelo Ramos lived his life fully, enjoying every moment. I lived mine in fear and anticipation of something terrible happening to me. As an adult, I know now that it was my grandmother who asked my grandfather to take us with him on his daily walks. She was suspicious that those morning walks were just a pretext for Abuelo Ramos visiting his girlfriends.

Our first stop, after buying a copy of his favorite newspaper, El ABC, was *El Círculo Mercantil e Industrial*, a very exclusive social club in Seville, where my grandfather was a longstanding member. It was a not-for-profit institution, not affiliated with any political party. To this day, I don't understand how a police detective became a member of the prestigious entity, but I have my theories. What I remember from the place was a friendly atmosphere. Everybody knew Abuelo Ramos. He was always greeted enthusiastically and with respect.

The club was located in the middle of one of the busiest streets in Seville, *La Calle Sierpe*, known for its high-end businesses, limited only to pedestrians. We used to sit outside the building, on rocking chairs, and watch people pass while my grandfather read his newspaper and chatted with other members.

On the way home, he would sing a folk song with us from his native Catalonia:

> *Baixant de la font del gat*
> *Una noia, una noia.*
> *Baixant de la font del gat*
> *Una noia i un soldat.*
> *Pregunteu-li com se diu:*

Marieta, Marieta!
Pregunteu-li com se diu:
Marieta del ull viu.
Marieta del ull viu.

I imagine he must have missed his homeland, resigned to living away from it in Franco's Spain—physically and emotionally.

After my Tia Lola passed, life for me in Sevilla became more difficult, so I cherished the time with my grandfather even more. My relationship with my father, on the other hand, was precarious at best.

My father was taking his second crack at medical school. He had caroused his way out of a spot in his first medical school class in Paris. Abuela Candida refused to suffer a drop-out for a son-in-law, so she pushed my father to try again, this time in Cadiz, about an hour south of Seville. My father was a very stubborn man who always did everything his way, without too much consideration for the well-being of others, including his family.

For her part, my mother could become agitated and self-absorbed without warning. She had an increasingly noticeable smoking habit. It was also around this time that I first noticed she and my grandparents favored my oldest brother, Juan Luis. He was proper, handsome, and intelligent, tall, and skinny—almost the opposite of me. I felt like he could do no wrong, and I made him pay for it.

On one occasion, my brother and I walked with my parents to a beautiful park, El Parque de Maria Luisa, on a gorgeous Sunday morning. As we strolled by the pristine gardens, I pushed my brother into a small grove of cactuses. My brother's skin was pierced through his clothes by the sharp thorns. My mother had to remove them one by one in the taxi on our way back home. It was a painful experience for my brother. This incident was the beginning of a series of personal attacks I issued against him. The tenor of our relationship didn't help matters at home.

My family's predispositions to mental illness and their sometimes cruel treatment toward me were heavily influenced by the violence they experienced and witnessed as small children during the Spanish Civil War and the Franco Regime.

They may even have inherited epigenetic "memories" from their parents and grandparents who saw the worst parts of the fighting, telling them that the world was an inherently violent, dangerous place. And I inherited the legacy of that anxiety—both from my parents' behavior toward me and, likely, in my genes.

Scientists have shown how specific genes and biological systems affect our stress responses, and the likelihood that we will develop anxiety, depression, or panic disorders. They've even shown how these genes can be turned "up" or "down" in laboratory mice whose parents have experienced stress and trauma.

Scientists now know that our thoughts, feelings, and actions are regulated by chemical messengers, which deliver messages from one cell to another in our bodies. Our bodies use these chemical messengers to transmit information from our five senses to our emotional brains, and from our emotional brains to the rest of our bodies.

When these messengers only travel between neurons, they're called neurotransmitters, and when they circulate to send messages throughout the body in the blood, they're called hormones. Differences in these neurotransmitters and hormones can explain why some people jump and become anxious at loud noises, while others nod.

They also explain why we feel butterflies in our stomach, why our heart races when we are scared, why chronic stress can affect our blood sugar and blood pressure, and other physical responses to thoughts and feelings that are played out in our bodies.

Scientists have now shown that in laboratory mice, many of these chemicals are released and processed differently because of our trauma and our parents' trauma. Early life trauma can affect how lab mice release and process serotonin, noradrenaline, glutamate, and corticotropin-releasing-factor—all chemicals that can cause or amplify certain emotions and thoughts.[5]

---

5   Holmes, A., Guisquet, A. M. L., Vogel, E., Millstein, R. A., Leman, S., & Belzung,

Research in humans shows us that similar epigenetic changes to the body's use of stress hormones and mood-altering chemicals happen in humans who experience early childhood trauma.[6] Science has also shown that these epigenetic changes can predict a person's likelihood of developing major depression or PTSD.[7]

This means that we must be gentle with ourselves. While we may desire to get rid of our anxiety or depression quickly or may even feel angry or disappointed with ourselves for feeling bad, these symptoms are caused by experiences we had no control over. They may also be influenced by the experiences our parents had before we were even born.

C. (2005). Early life genetic, epigenetic and environmental factors shaping emotionality in rodents. *Neuroscience & Biobehavioral Reviews, 29*(8), 1335–1346. doi: 10.1016/j.neubiorev.2005.04.012

6   Hing, B., Gardner, C., & Potash, J. B. (2014). Effects of negative stressors on DNA methylation in the brain: Implications for mood and anxiety disorders. *American Journal of Medical Genetics Part B: Neuropsychiatric Genetics, 165*(7), 541–554. doi: 10.1002/ajmg.b.32265

7   Klengel, T., Pape, J., Binder, E. B., & Mehta, D. (2014). The role of DNA methylation in stress-related psychiatric disorders. *Neuropharmacology, 80*, 115–132. doi: 10.1016/j.neuropharm.2014.01.013

CHAPTER 5

ON AN ISLAND

AS I TURNED six years old, my family left Spain for Puerto Rico, where my dad's family lived. At first, my mother looked forward to the change. Her own mother was hard on her, and she was hoping to take a break from the constant anxiety of pleasing Abuela Candida and meeting all her expectations. My grandmother was controlling and overprotective of my mom. I don't think my mom felt loved and accepted for who she really was. My grandmother was intrusive with her own social expectations for my mother, imposing on her challenging roles that interfered with mom's ability to be who she really was. Abuela Candida believed it was my mother's responsibility to meet all her needs at the expense of my mother's desires.

But Puerto Rico proved to be an anxiety-filled setting for the rest of my mother's life. The frequent thunderstorms and the annual threat of hurricanes tormented her for decades on the island. I think she viewed her suffering as penance for leaving her parents behind.

My mother came to regret that after her parents had raised her in Spain almost like a queen, she could end up in a foreign country, regarded as a simple and insignificant maid in a household brimming with lunatics. My dad was unsupportive and distant. He was lazy—an astrology fanatic who relied on empty prayers to the Blessed Virgin Mary and spent more time in bed than in the office.

Nobody in the house looked after my mother. For my paternal grandparents, she was another house servant. They treated her like an intruder.

Puerto Rico is a world away from Seville in several respects. The island is a commonwealth of the United States. The population is an ethnic mix of Spanish descendants, black Africans, and native Indians called Tainos. Spanish is the official language, and the culture is a lot like any other country in Latin America, but Puerto Ricans are also native-born American citizens and the hallmarks of Americana render a unique mélange.

In 1961, our family hero, President John F. Kennedy, visited the island. Three years prior, he had visited Puerto Rico as a Democratic senator running for President of the United States. The campaign invited my paternal grandfather to attend on both occasions.

My Puerto Rican grandfather, Don Luis Torres Diaz, was a respected scholar and the Dean of the University of the Puerto Rico School of Pharmacy, which he had helped to establish. He was an essential figure in the university and he had some political powers and connections. The island elites respected him. He was a close ally of the governor, Don Luis Muñoz Marín. He supported the U.S. Democratic Party and was a vigorous proponent of protecting the Commonwealth of Puerto Rico.

Abuelo Luis believed President Kennedy was a loyal friend of Puerto Rico. The fascination with Kennedy is one of the few traits shared by the two sides of my family tree, and I'm convinced that the overlap has an outsized role in my own fascination with the Kennedy family.

After we came to Puerto Rico we moved in with my paternal grandparents, whom I had only met once before. Their house, to me, was like a haunted mansion. It was all foreign to me.

My paternal grandmother, Doña Emma Luisa Vidal, was a stay-at-home mother. After she lost her first child when he was still an infant her entire world changed. She blamed herself for having left the child in the care of a nanny while she and my grandfather went to a university social gala. After his unexpected and painful death, she was never the same, and both my father and my uncle suffered the consequences. They had to be raised by their own grandmother.

One thing I noticed the first time I went into Abuela Emma's bedroom was the picture of Jiddu Krishnamurti on her nightstand. She didn't have any photographs of my grandfather. Krishnamurti was an Indian philosopher. He spoke of psychological revolution, the need to meditate and test human relationships. He wrote against cultural norms and described the mind and consciousness in cosmic terms. It would have scandalized my grandparents in Spain to see his portrait on the nightstand of my Puerto Rican grandmother's room.

In Spain, my grandparents led a relatively humble life. In Puerto Rico, things were different. My Puerto Rican family employed a housemaid named Pepa, who took care of all the daily household chores. Our rooms were on the second floor of a stand-alone house, but my parents' bedroom was just a door away from our bedroom.

Under the staircase, there was a small and uncomfortable walk-in closet where my parents used to punish me when I didn't behave. Pepa had a disgusting body odor, a nauseating stink that settled in my nostrils for days after she was gone, but when I sensed it coming near, I knew I was safe. She used to let me out of the closet sometimes.

My father was around more often in Puerto Rico than he had been in Spain, but that did not prove to be a comfort. He was self-absorbed, obsessed with his own fantasies, and always at odds with his demanding, and much more successful, father.

This Abuelo was a prominent figure in Puerto Rico—an author and founder of the School of Pharmacy at the University of Puerto Rico. His son was a disappointment, having barely graduated from medical school and practicing as a psychiatrist for the Veterans' Administration without ever getting board certification in the field.

Once we moved to Puerto Rico, I struggled more with my anxiety—meeting unfamiliar people, addressing my identity, competing with my brother, reacting to my parents. I took things personally when they were talking about me. I felt them comparing me to my brother and using his successes to highlight how unlike him I was.

In psychology and psychiatry, some mental health conditions appear to happen *only* within particular cultures. This can be a challenge for patients and doctors alike, as doctors without cross-cultural training may not identify the cause or the best treatment for a patient's distress if the patient is suffering from a culture-specific syndrome not familiar with. No one quite knows why culture-specific syndromes happen, but culture-specific beliefs may cause them. Distinct cultures may hold unique views about self-control, free will, good or evil spirits, and the nature of human thoughts, emotions, and sexuality, to name a few. These beliefs may then cause culturally-specific fears, anxieties, behaviors, and delusions. These conditions may be widely accepted as a natural consequence of one culture's worldview but considered baffling, illegitimate, or fake in another culture that does not share the same views about the world and human nature.

The concept of an *ataque de nervios* is prevalent in Latino culture specifically. As described, symptoms are like those of a panic attack accompanied by uncontrollable screaming, shouting, or crying dissociative experiences, and aggressive behavior.[8] These additional features of dissociation and senses of being out of control to distinguish these attacks from the diagnosable psychiatric condition.[9] The underlying belief seems to be that people may experience overpowering emotional pain and loss of control over their actions when overwhelmed with emotional distress.

To make matters more complicated, scientists believe that variables including "acceptance of negative emotions,"[10] "family discord

---

8   Koydemir, S., & Essau, C. A. (2018). Anxiety and Anxiety Disorders in Young People. *Understanding Uniqueness and Diversity in Child and Adolescent Mental Health*, 115–134. DOI: 10.1016/b978-0-12-815310-9.00005-8

9   DSM Glossary of Cultural Concepts of Distress: Ataques de Nervios. (n.d.). Retrieved from https://dsm.psychiatryonline.org/doi/10.1176/appi.books.9780890425596.GlossaryofCulturalConceptsofDistress

10   Viana, A. G., Paulus, D. J., Bakhshaie, J., Garza, M., Valdivieso, J., Ochoa-Perez, M.,… Zvolensky, M. J. (2017). Emotional nonacceptance within the context of traumatic event

and cohesion,"[11] and neurological sensitivity to pain,[12] which is affected by both past trauma and genetic factors, may play roles in how people respond to emotional distress.

This raises the genuine possibility that cultures, with different beliefs and practices regarding the proper way to experience or express emotions, may give rise to biologically and psychologically various manifestations of anxiety and emotional distress.

Culture is not limited to nation-states or civilizations. Workplaces and schools have distinct cultures. So do families.

The culture of anxiety and judgment I encountered in Puerto Rico was unlike anything I had experienced in Spain. I could feel the pressure in my bones, and I lived for a long time on the brink of an *ataque de nervios* like the one described in the anthropological literature. I was probably more susceptible because of my underlying genetics and previous discreet experiences with anxiety-like my fear of drowning.

I struggled in elementary school on the island. My second-grade teacher told my parents they would not promote me to the third grade because of my poor grades and my disruptive classroom behavior. That's when Sister Marjolein, a Bernardine Franciscan nun, entered my life. Her vocation as a missionary and teacher made her the perfect person to rescue me from myself. She accepted it as a personal quest to make me a better student.

Sister Marjolein knew that I didn't like to speak English, but to make things worse, she didn't speak any Spanish. However, she was persistent and used her pedagogical techniques to get me to talk to

---

exposure: The critical role of anxiety sensitivity for traumatic stress symptoms and disability among Latinos in a primary care setting. *General Hospital Psychiatry, 44,* 30–37. DOI: 10.1016/j.genhosppsych.2016.10.007

11 Priest, J. B., & Denton, W. (2012). Anxiety Disorders and Latinos. *Hispanic Journal of Behavioral Sciences, 34*(4), 557–575. DOI: 10.1177/0739986312459258

12 Bakhshaie, J., Kauffman, B. Y., Viana, A. G., Garza, M., Ochoa-Perez, M., Lemaire, C.,... Zvolensky, M. J. (2017). Synergistic effects of pain intensity and experiential avoidance concerning anxiety symptoms and disorders among economically disadvantaged Latinos in a community-based primary care setting. *Journal of Anxiety Disorders, 48,* 54–62. DOI: 10.1016/j.janxdis.2016.08.004

her in English. I enjoyed my time alone with her. She had a beautiful round face with rosy cheeks. Her hands were soft. She used to rub my head every time I did something right.

Sister Marjolein became a mother figure to me. She spent hours after school teaching me math and science. I remember her playing records on an old record player about God and how He created the universe. We sang the songs together until I memorized the lyrics.

First, God created the Heaven and the Earth
And when He saw His creation was worth
He said: Good, good, very, very good.
Very good, said the Lord.
Sing glory alleluia, a wonderful sight to see.
Sing glory alleluia, that's how it came to be.

I enjoyed those moments, and it was the first time that I felt a special connection with God. I felt loved and cared for.

Many years later, I would receive the terrible news that Sister Marjolein had been murdered while on a mission in Zimbabwe, known then as Rhodesia. Another personal loss in my life that still, to this day, is painful to remember.

We spent every summer back in Spain with my mom's family, and every year I was reluctant to return to school in Puerto Rico. I would beg my parents not to send me back.

One morning I got into an argument with my parents just before we were ready to go out in the car. Like I always did, I shut down and refused to talk to them. They decided not to put up with my behavior, and they both got in the car and drove off.

I tried to run behind the car, crying and begging them to stop and to wait for me, but they kept going. I ran to the street, following the Falcon's rear red lights until Pepa pulled me inside the house. She had witnessed all the action and was ready to offer her wise advice and comfort.

She reminded me that if I wanted to be happy in life, I had to hurry and mature faster than my brother. She sensed that my parents would not wait for me to catch up with my emotional development.

Many years later, I continued to be terrified that the car would depart at any moment without me, taking my parents and leaving me behind.

Despite Pepa's advice, I continued to struggle and act out at school. I felt lesser than my brother Juan Luis, who breezed through classes, always the teacher's favorite. I remember many instances when I was compared to my brother by my teachers. They questioned my relationship with him. "Are you sure you're related?" they would tease me.

Every weekday afternoon, my brother and I rushed home from school to watch our favorite television program: *Cine Recreo con Pacheco*. The host, Pacheco, was a Spanish comedian from Barcelona. After years in Cuba, he had escaped Castro's revolution, and in 1962 WAPA-TV hired him. His actual name was Joaquin Monserrat.

In the program, Pacheco gave children advice. He interviewed entertaining local guests and played cartoons. One of the show's unique characteristics was the regular display of drawings submitted by children across the island who watched the show.

Often, as he was showing the chosen drawing to the TV audience, naming the child and describing the image, Pacheco would interject a message from *un pajarito investigador* (a little messenger birdie) recounting something terrible about the child's behavior that needed to be corrected.

Every weekday, when the clock read 3 p.m., I was already seated in front of the TV with a box of Kellogg's Frosted Flakes and a bowl of milk in my hands, waiting for this hypnotizing figure with a unique white Buster Keaton hat and a classic bow tie to appear. It was an opportunity for a little guy like me to connect with other children who wanted to be heard.

I sent a drawing once a week, hoping to appear on camera. I had been sending at least one drawing per week since I started watching the show. I was trying to get Pacheco's attention and get him to know me by submitting my drawings. I wanted his approval and acknowledgment. For the drawings, I always chose a picture of our house and myself. Sometimes I included our car and a sketch of me with my parents.

I remember one day when he pulled out one of my drawings at the end of the show. I couldn't believe it. It overwhelmed me with excitement and joy. But my mood changed quickly.

Pacheco started reading from the back of my drawing. Pacheco whispered in a serious voice that a *pajarito investigador* had told him I was not behaving. I was hurting my older brother, Pacheco said. In a very emphatic and stern tone of voice, he offered his usual advice for this sort of situation.

He said, "When you hurt your brother, you hurt your parents and all your loved ones. You also hurt yourself by not letting your big brother take care of you, protecting you from the outside world. The family should always be united and supportive of each other."

At first, I thought it was a frightful dream—a nightmare. Then I got scared and fled to my mother, telling her what had just happened. She told me that Jesus had reported me to Pacheco. From that moment on, I promised God I would be useful and never again hurt my brother.

Of course, this promise lasted a few weeks at most. A handful of Saturdays later, my parents took us to visit some friends in the country. My youngest sister was almost 3 years old, and they strapped her into the back seat, between my brother and me. It excited me we were all going in the car to a new place. Since my sister was born, I had resented the attention she enjoyed from my family.

After an uneventful two-hour car drive, we arrived at the house we were visiting. It was nestled in the middle of a large lot, covered with beautiful red *flamboyanes*, my favorite tree. The flowers of the *flamboyán* are large, with red petals. For the Indians of Kerala, the *flamboyán* is the "flower of Calvary." It is believed that when Jesus was crucified, His blood was shed over its flowers, and this is how the petals got their characteristic bright red color.

Once we parked, my mother told us she and my dad would go inside with my sister. My mother instructed my oldest brother to remain with me in the car until they were back. She reminded him not to let me leave the automobile.

I was angry they had taken my sister and left us behind. The gnawing feeling of abandonment got me agitated. I moved into the front seat. As usual, my brother stuck his nose in a book he had lugged with him for the trip. My mom had told him he was to ensure I behaved.

Without Juan Luis noticing, I pushed in the cigarette lighter to make it hot. The moment it popped out of its socket, I grabbed it surreptitiously before unleashing it on my brother. I tried to burn him on his chest and arms—the hot metal seared black holes into his shirt. I was mad at my parents, but I took it out on him. Out of desperation, my brother took his shirt off to use it as a shield to protect himself.

Because my brother was afraid I might get hurt if he left me inside the car by myself, he didn't try to abandon the vehicle. When my parents arrived 30 minutes later, they found my brother with what I left of his shirt in his hands. He had several burns on his arms and chest.

My mother's reaction was uncharacteristic. Instead of reprimanding me, she started yelling at my brother for not being able to control me. I went back to the rear seat without saying a word. I could see my dad laughing at my brother, condescending to his perceived weakness. To this day, I have to admit that the memory of that incident brings me a perverse sense of misguided pride.

Years later, I learned that my brother and mom were the ones who wrote the story of my misdeeds on the back of the drawing for Pacheco.

In the past, my brother had tried his hand unsuccessfully at different non-violent solutions for my selfish and violent behavior toward him. He even advised the school priest not to grant me my first communion. He thought the fear of not making communion would change my ways. As usual, I carried on inflicting physical pain. Communion be damned, I guess.

Sometime later, my mother got me into becoming an altar server, like my brother was, to get me to behave correctly. I met this attempt with defiance too.

However, Pacheco was different. Ever since we moved to Puerto Rico, the person I missed the most from Spain was my Abuelo Ramos. Pacheco was from Catalonia, just like my grandfather. His accent and demeanor reminded me of Abuelo Ramos. I trusted him and always felt calm and mesmerized when I watched his show and heard him speak. Unbeknownst to Pacheco, he had a powerful influence over me.

Despite my connection with Pacheco, my fears and anxieties continued to torment me. I tried to find peace and solitude with my Puerto Rican grandfather to no avail. He was preoccupied with his duties at the university and his writings. Even though he seemed to care about me in his own way, I could not see myself opening up to him.

One day he offered me a chance to accompany him to Washington, D.C., where he was receiving a prestigious award in front of thousands of people. He didn't ask my brother or my dad. He made me feel unique and significant. It would be my first visit to the United States. I was willing to overcome my fear of separation from my mother to travel with my famous grandfather.

I will never forget the advice my Abuelo Luis gave me on our three-hour flight. He said, "Kiko, if you want to be successful in life, you have to behave at all times like if you were a public figure." I didn't fully appreciate the value of his words then, but I have carried them in my mind ever since. Part of my disappointment with myself has been my failure to follow this advice.

CHAPTER 6

SUMMER OF '69

I GREW UP afraid. When I was a young child I lost sleep, panicked by the prospect of change. Our house was one of those where the sounds of the television filled in the silence of our lives. The voices of news anchors and politicians arguing over the military draft were like echoes that haunted me every day.

At nine years of age, the thought they might draft me to fight in Vietnam petrified me. I presume this was the reason I became interested at such an early stage in my life in prominent public figures opposing the draft like Dr. Martin Luther King and the famous boxer, Muhammad Ali.

Like the song, I vividly recall the summer of 1969. That year, we had the moon landing, the climax of the Vietnam War, the free love of Woodstock, Mohamed Ali banned from the boxing ring because of his opposition to the draft, and serial killers Charles Manson and the Zodiac Killer.

Robert Kennedy and Martin Luther King, Jr. had been murdered just one year prior. It was an age of political, civil, and personal unrest.

In 1968, I used to watch a popular American police television series called "The FBI." I used to watch it with my parents. We would gather around the television set in the living room.

The show chronicled a group of FBI agents seeking to defend the US Government from various threats. They based the series on actual FBI cases. Some episodes ended with the most wanted criminal of the day. Efrem Zimbalist, Jr., who played Inspector Lewis Erskine in the series, was the host for this piece.

I always awaited this real-life epilogue with great anticipation. For me, this was a fascinating part of the show. But it also struck fear in me from time to time.

I will never forget the episode which aired on April 21, 1968. In this episode, Zimbalist, Jr. asked for information about a fugitive named James Earl Ray. Ray was being hunted at the time for the murder of Dr. Martin Luther King, Jr., who had been shot and killed the evening of April 4, 1968. Even though at the time I was seven years old, I felt the same way I felt when Kennedy was gunned down.

My family raised us in a strong pro-Democratic Party atmosphere, even though Puerto Ricans couldn't vote for president. They were in favor of the civil rights movement, which Kennedy had promoted.

When they murdered Dr. King, my father related this to a CIA conspiracy, just like he did when they killed President Kennedy. After Robert Kennedy was shot and killed a few months later, a sense of dread and paranoia invaded the family and me. Conspiracy talk was in the air.

The summer of 1969 was also when doctors in Spain diagnosed Abuelo Ramos with liver cirrhosis. The disease was most likely related to chronic alcohol consumption. My parents never informed me of the specifics about his condition, but by looking at my mom's face and her demeanor, I could tell it was something serious.

My mother had to scrape money together to travel more regularly to Spain. The international phone calls multiplied each month, far outpacing the usual once a week long-distance call on Sundays. I didn't understand what was taking place, but I missed my grandfather more often than usual. My mother became gloomy and agitated.

On August 8 and 9, 1969, just a few days after we had returned from Spain, we heard on the television the news about the disciples of cult leader Charles Manson, who had driven into a wealthy community in Los Angeles and slaughtered seven people, seemingly at random. Among them was an actress, Sharon Tate, eight months pregnant.

The murders captured the American imagination. Charles Manson manipulated and weaponized young women to carry out his objectives of destabilizing the American socio-political structure. The nature of the crimes captivated my family. My parents became obsessed with the gross details and the pictures shown daily on the television.

Before the summer of 1969, every Sunday afternoon I relaxed with my grandparents on the house's front balcony and monitored passersby. Occasionally a neighbor would come in and join the conversation. The front porch was spacious, with a small unlocked gate separating the house from the road. I cherished my conversations there with Abuelo Luis.

He used to regale me with stories of his early life in the country, and also about when he moved to San Juan to start his studies to become a Doctor of Pharmacy. His knowledge and his manner of speaking fascinated me. He carefully said every word, paying close attention to its pronunciation. He firmly believed the only correct Spanish dialect was Castilian.

One day in late August, the world inside our television set materialized right before my eyes. I didn't recognize my house. They caged the spacious porch where I spent afternoons with my grandfather with white iron bars. The family had installed a wide gate between the front lawn and the front door. Nobody warned me the change was coming.

I felt like I was entering prison or a birdcage. I suspected that the Manson family crimes had inspired the security measures. They'd erected iron bars to keep the world at bay. I feared it would keep us isolated too.

The separation spoiled my afternoons on the porch. Trapped

behind the iron gates, I felt like I was drowning, like the air was trapped outside. It was claustrophobic. I was manic about monitoring whoever had the keys.

The year 1969 was also when the United States put a man on the moon—eight years after President Kennedy had vowed to do it in a speech to Congress. The government had poured millions of dollars into NASA's Apollo missions. By the spring of 1969, NASA had the technology necessary to reach the moon, but safety was a concern.

Based on the calculations made by the crew of the Apollo 10 mission, there would be a one-hour period during the lunar module orbit when the crew would be unable to communicate with Mission Control. They would be lost on the dark side of the moon. This would be one of the most dangerous parts of the mission.

The teacher told us about it at school. The fear that we would lose the astronauts kept me up at night. I would wake up in a sweat and run to my parents' room or wake up my brother.

On July 16, 1969, the Apollo 11 rockets lifted off. Four days later, on July 20, the lunar module landed on a wide flat area of the moon called The Sea of Tranquility. A few hours later, Neil Armstrong became the first person to walk on the moon. I remember the excitement at the house and school. The black and white televisions were always on, awaiting images from space.

Other children used the opportunity to tell tales about encounters with aliens and UFOs. Their stories would unsettle me. My father brought home books of extraterrestrial life and encounters with "Martians." Despite his strong religious convictions, he believed we were not alone, and he spouted off frequently about the existence of sophisticated extraterrestrial beings in space.

He referred to the Burned Memo, a document which hinted that the CIA had a hand in Kennedy's death not because Kennedy was weak on Communism or his war against crime, but because he wanted to reveal the truth about what the American government knew about UFOs. He might as well have been telling me ghost stories in a tent. It terrified me.

Over the next few years, Abuelo Ramos' medical condition deteriorated. In 1972 my grandmother called my mother crying and begging her to come back home as soon as possible. Abuelo was dying. It was December, and my mother wanted to wait until we were out of school for the holidays before leaving.

She was planning on taking us with her for those few weeks to say goodbye to Abuelo Ramos and, if necessary, she would send us back home alone, so she could stay with her dad. Just the thought of us coming back alone in an airplane terrified me. I wasn't afraid of flying, but of terrorist hijackings—another byproduct of the television set.

My family's fretting over world events was not cabined to 1969. We lived in constant fear of the outside world. Some causes of this distress were very real. The United States had used nuclear weapons against Japan, and no one was sure that the U.S. or Soviets wouldn't use them on each other's cities in the near future. The American government discussed putting civil rights leaders and anti-war activists on watch lists and considered ways to discredit them and break up their followings.[13]

At the same time, some of the global anxiety was unjustified hysteria. The "satanic panic" that caused most Americans to believe it was an undeniable fact that rampant Satanic cults were abusing children and carrying out ritual murders turned out to be based almost entirely on false claims and wild speculation.[14] Watching too much TV almost seems quaint nowadays. But the challenge mass media poses to those of us prone to anxiety was as real in the '60s and '70s as it is today.[15] Even then, news agencies discovered they could increase their ad revenue by sensationalizing stories and reporting unsubstantiated claims of Satanic violence. Political parties found that

---

13   Federal Bureau of Investigation (FBI). (2018, May 21). Retrieved from https://kinginstitute.stanford.edu/encyclopedia/federal-bureau-investigation-fbi

14   Shewan, D. (2015, September 8). Conviction of Things Not Seen: The Uniquely American Myth of Satanic Cults. Retrieved from https://psmag.com/social-justice/make-a-cross-with-your-fingers-its-the-satanic-panic

15   Jackson, J. (2019). *You are what you read: why changing your media diet can change the world*. London: Unbound.

they could gain support by claiming that their opponents were threats to national security. My family lived in times when dangerous events were happening—but they were probably also needlessly anxious about things that were not likely to affect them directly in any way.

Today, the effect of media on mental health has only intensified. Anyone can circulate sensational stories to everyone else, all over the world, all at once. The science is in—we are addicted to social media, and social media causes anxiety. It's a perfect storm.

As I entered the 1970s, my anxiety was building, and our family addiction to the news didn't help.

CHAPTER 7
SPANISH CHRISTMAS

WE BOOKED OUR trip to Spain to start the first day of our school's Christmas break. Although the primary purpose of the trip was to say the last goodbye to Abuelo Ramos, I was excited. The last Christmas I spent in Seville was when I was five years old.

My mind was teeming with fond memories, most of them with Abuelo Ramos. I was also excited about flying and returning to the family I preferred—my mom's. My dad wasn't coming with us this time, and that was fine with me.

Unfortunately, I wasn't immune to my mom's anxiety and growing sense of grief. I don't recall seeing her without a cigarette in her hands during the entire flight. In 1972, the tail end of the "golden years of flying," you could still smoke inside the plane, as long as you were seated in the designated smoking section, the last five or six rows.

I always found it baffling how they separated the plane between smokers and non-smokers when the air we all were breathing was circulating inside the entire cabin. Someone once compared this to having a separate section in the pool for urinating. I recall reading at the time, "cigarette smoke hides the smell of fear." Not even the cigarette smoke filling the cabin could hide my mom's.

I was miserable for the entire eight hours it took to arrive in Madrid. In those days, traveling by plane was pricey. There were no options, and just a few airlines controlled the air space. My parents had to take a loan to pay for this unscheduled trip. That alone amplified my mother's anxiety.

Flying in the '70s was deemed a luxury and restricted to a few well-to-do families or celebrities. That doesn't mean flying was necessarily fun, particularly for a 12-year-old kid. There were no in-flight movies. You had to make do with a book or a magazine from home. When you sat in your assigned airplane seat, the flight attendant brought you a postcard with a picture of the plane to scribble on the back of and send it to your friends and family informing them about your trip. That was the sole form of entertainment the airline provided.

That said, the meals were luxurious and included all the drinks you could want—including unlimited alcoholic drinks too. On one of our summer trips, I recall how they unloaded a drunk passenger on a stretcher through the plane.

My father, traveling with us, had hidden behind his front seat as the flight attendant asked through the plane's speaker if there was a physician in the cabin. He became distressed and, in a way, paranoid. He was always scared of divulging to anybody he was a medical doctor. His excuse was that he didn't want to induce any harm, but we all felt that the actual reason was his fear of a medical negligence lawsuit. His fear was contagious, and I am ashamed to admit that I thought the same way early in my medical career. Thankfully, I overcame that particular inheritance.

Our wait in Madrid for our connecting flight to Seville was brief. Once we landed in Seville, we took a taxi and went straight to the old family home. Our apartment was on the third floor, and there was no elevator. In those days in Spain, there was no concern for individuals with physical impairments.

We had to take our baggage to the top using the cramped staircase. Once we arrived at the apartment, Abuela Candida was waiting for us in the corridor. She wept inconsolably while she gave each one of us lots of kisses and hugs. Just behind her was Tia Pilar, excitedly anticipating her turn with us.

Inside the apartment was all gloom and sorrow. We went straight to the room Abuelo Ramos was using during his illness. When he looked at us, his eyes instantly lit up and grew fuller. You could see the color coming back to his face, especially when he saw my mom. My mother and Abuelo Ramos had a profoundly emotional encounter without exchanging a single word.

In the interim, my Abuela and Tia Pilar took us to the kitchen to have something to eat. They showed us our sleeping arrangements, and from that time on, their mission was to protect us from the melancholy filling the apartment. They fed us mounds of exquisite Spanish food and tempting sweets.

Christmas in Seville was so different from in Puerto Rico. You could sense the Holy Spirit everywhere you went, including the stores. I relished the smell of chestnuts, or castañas as we call them, crackling over open flames. In Spain, the birth of Jesus was the focus, as well as the joy and happiness of children. Church activities were a priority, and we went to Mass often. Besides all that, the weather was wintry, and we had to suit up accordingly.

The home was always busy with visitors who showed up to see how Abuelo Ramos was doing. The local church pastor visited the apartment every evening and spent better than an hour with us, mainly with Abuelo. My grandma and aunt always prepared something to eat, including the regular bottle of Spanish red wine, so emblematic of our culture.

The priest's name was Padre Enrique, and he was my mother's age. I recall his grin and benevolence. He was always extremely polite and friendly to us. When he entered Abuelo's chamber, he always locked the door behind him. Even though at the time I didn't understand particularly well, Padre Enrique was presenting him with the sacrament of confession.

I couldn't understand why Abuelo Ramos had to confess. I always saw him as a pure human being with no defects. It never crossed my mind that a man so loving and caring could ever do something demanding the mercy of God.

Every time I entered Abuelo's room to visit with him, there was a picture hanging on the wall behind the bed, which turned into a nightmare for me. It was a copy of an oil painting by Raphael, the famous Sistine Madonna. It captured the Virgin Mary with baby Jesus in her arms. The actual painting is renowned for the state of religious ecstasy it provokes in onlookers. Many have described the physical effects of staring at it—elevated heart rates, fainting, confusion, even hallucinations. Famous artists cite their influence by the painting, including Goethe, Wagner, Nietzsche, and even Dostoyevsky.

My grandmother herself asserted that if you stared at the Virgin Mary's eyes and tried to walk around the room, her eyes would seek you out wherever you go. The Virgin Mary stared at me even when the room was darkened.

Abuela used this well-established optical phenomenon to plant a seed in my youthful mind, the image of being watched by the Virgin Mary wherever I went. She felt it was a convenient way of forcing me to behave. To this day, the thought of the Madonna painting continues to evoke a rise in my heartbeat with occasional giddiness and anxiety.

After spending two great weeks in Spain with the family, the time came to leave. I said my sad goodbyes to Abuelo Ramos, not knowing this would be the last time I would ever see him. My family never told me how sick he indeed was. They didn't reveal the fact that he had merely a few more weeks to live. I must have sensed it a little though, I think.

I won't ever forget those goodbyes. Abuelo gave me his blessing, and he encouraged me to study hard so I could become a prominent gentleman. His face read love and care and happiness. I left the room under the watchful gaze of the Madonna, tears welling in my eyes.

We flew back home on January 3, 1973. The new year was already in progress. The flight was tedious, and I was glad that they gave me the window seat. I already missed my mother and Abuelo. She had stayed behind with her dad.

I continued staring through the window for most of the flight, except for when we were served dinner or breakfast. I assumed I could sleep for a few hours. When the captain announced that we were 20 miles from Puerto Rico, I focused my attention on trying to locate the island as quickly as we were close enough. I recall the excitement when I saw the tiny houses and the coastline.

As we descended, I could identify landmarks. The first was El Morro Castle, which was sitting majestically on the westside of El Viejo San Juan. I realized then we were very close to the runway and about to land. I made sure that I secured my seatbelt, and my seat was in the vertical position.

When the plane started its final approach, I saw through the window something unexpected. There were several Coast Guard helicopters flying above Isla Verde Beach and over five ships in the water. A considerable crowd of people was observing from the shore.

A passenger behind me remarked that they were still looking for Roberto Clemente's aircraft. I never heard the news while in Spain of the airplane accident and the death of my favorite baseball star, Roberto Clemente. He had been killed on New Year's Eve, a few miles from the airfield, while traveling on a mission to distribute supplies to the earthquake-stricken people of Nicaragua.

When I learned of his death, my chest grew tight, and I could hear my heartbeat thumping in my ears. The sense of loss was overwhelming. Just three weeks later, we received the news of Abuelo Ramos' death.

CHAPTER 8

DAZED AND CONFUSED

MY STRUGGLES IN grade school were well documented by the time I got to sixth grade. But this was when I would start to turn things around. I became a better student, hoping to earn a professional degree, eventually. But I also had to endure daily bullying by older students. I was overweight, with poor self-esteem. I was terrified but told no one about my fears.

At the end of each afternoon, while all the kids were happy to go home, panic and terror consumed me as the dismissal bell rang. I knew I had to walk through a long and dark hallway before reaching the school bus.

Almost every day I was confronted by ten high school seniors and juniors waiting behind the gate to attack me. They were widely feared on campus, and no one wanted to hang around to challenge them. They used their ties as sharp whips to strike my body, including my face. I was carrying a heavy military green backpack full of textbooks and could not move fast.

As they hit me, they were laughing and calling me names. "What's the matter, fat boy, your mom can't help you? Why are you crying? Does it hurt? Do you want us to stop?"

I wasn't equipped to react well. I couldn't tell my father, who I feared would humiliate me. I didn't trust the teachers. What I did instead was shameful. To normalize my mental chaos, I picked on a younger kid.

Cheito had just moved in across the street with his single mother, a younger brother, and his maternal grandparents. They lived on the top floor of a large two-story house with a spacious fenced balcony visible to me from my grandmother's bedroom terrace.

The house itself belonged to an older retired couple who were close friends of my grandparents. They rented portions of the house out to college students as a way to supplement their retirement income. I used to go over to their house often with my grandparents to stare at the beautiful young college co-eds and to spend time with them on the front porch. The young girls used to compliment me and tell me how adorable I was.

I met Cheito the day he moved in, while I was visiting the neighbors. He was a few years younger than me—bone-thin with jet-black overlong hair. When I saw his mom I recall my excitement and immediate infatuation. I recognized her from one of the local television soap operas my mom used to watch with me in the afternoons. I felt special to know someone important and so beautiful. She had an infectious grin and displayed an air of royalty and class. Her green eyes were striking. You could appreciate just by looking at her she was a celebrity.

Cheito's mother was an actress who had just recently signed a lucrative contract with one of the major local television producers. She grew up in an artistic household and she started acting professionally before she had even started school. Her behavior and her lifestyle were emblematic of the '60s. We all could see her two children playing naked on the balcony. Sometimes, she herself would appear outside topless to hang her wet clothes over the railing to dry. She was invariably in favor of just causes and fought for the conservation of the climate. Apart from being a free spirit, she was an idealist and a remarkably wise woman.

Occasionally, when she was away at work, my mother offered to babysit Cheito. I was constantly waiting every afternoon for the arrival to enjoy her brief presence in our house. But I started taunting and verbally harassing Cheito while he was at our house. As soon as my mother became distracted by a household chore, I started calling Cheito names. The one name which was the most hurtful to him was *Cucaracha* (cockroach). I called him "Cheito Cucaracha" until his eyes swelled up and became watery. My mom could sometimes stop my bullying once she noticed Cheito crying.

I have to concede I didn't feel remorseful about what I was doing at the time. I don't recall any specific motive; I just enjoyed seeing Cheito cry. I didn't care if he could tell his mother about what I was doing. Maybe I was trying to get Cheito's mom's attention, or maybe I was envious of him. I was handling my own unpleasant feelings by picking on a vulnerable kid, and I didn't feel bad about doing it.

Well, one day the unavoidable finally happened. On a Saturday morning, Cheito's mom came to the house asking to talk to me and my mother. She looked serious and disturbed. With a very gentle but firm voice, she started the conversation, talking about the psychological harm inflicted on children by bullies, although she didn't use that word. She just wanted to give me an opportunity to mend my behavior and to avoid doing this to other kids. From that day on, Cheito's visits to the house became less frequent.

I lived in fear of my own bullies at school until I reached the ninth grade and the seniors and juniors were gone. In my junior year of high school, after spending the summer as a volunteer at a private hospital emergency room, I decided I wanted to study medicine. I wanted to become a doctor, like my dad, maybe to get his attention or perhaps to prove to him and the family that I was capable of more than what they expected from me. I committed that I would make it into college and ultimately to medical school. I vowed my brother wouldn't be the only successful student.

CHAPTER 9

CARJACKED

ONCE I GOT to college, I studied hard. But I didn't get into medical school on my first try. I was devastated, ready to accept my failed destiny. I felt lost and uncertain of what I could be in the world.

The woman who would become my wife, someone who had grown up without the anxieties and insecurities I faced, helped me to find myself, to study harder, and to get me into medical school the next year. She had already been accepted and was already very successful and popular among her peers.

I met Elvira during our first year of college. Before that, I never had a girlfriend. My experience with girls my age was minimal. I was timid and awkward. She was the one who started talking to me and showing some interest in developing a relationship. My dating skills were primitive and unpolished. I don't know how we started dating, but the fact is that I fell in love.

I felt loved and appreciated. We had most of our classes together. We both wanted to become physicians. We became inseparable.

I don't remember having too many close male friends, but we both belonged to a very selective group of students called *El Grupo de Los Cien*. They chose the group of one hundred students every year from the top high school class on the island to finish undergraduate education in three years before applying to medical school.

But I wasn't so lucky. I had to remain in college for my fourth year and get a part-time job doing medical research in the middle of El Viejo San Juan. I took three public buses and walked four miles one way three times a week to get to work. Meanwhile, there was chaos at the University of Puerto Rico. A group of well-organized students went on strike.

These were trying times for me, attending classes in the middle of violent protests, including explosions and shootings. I worried they would cancel the current academic year and force me to wait another year before reapplying to medical school.

In 1980, the University had increased the salaries of the president and the chancellors by upwards of 40 percent. Rumors spread that tuition would increase, and in 1981, under the administration of pro-statehood party Gov. Romero Barceló, tuition fees were increased for all students.

The vast majority of students organized against the tuition hikes. The media expected violence—it would not have been the first time the UPR served as the setting for violent political confrontation. During the independence movements of the '50s and '60s, the university was the epicenter of the fight.

The chancellor implemented a series of mediating committees and banned meetings, marches, and picketing on the Rio Piedras campus, where I was a student. Several students were arrested and expelled for protesting. The SWAT and riot police operated on campus as students occupied classroom buildings.

Support for the movement was growing—the tuition hikes were seen as unfair to lower-income students who relied on government-funded education for social mobility and economic opportunity. The organized protests and the general strike grew beyond the original leftist agitators and swelled to a multitude. The confrontations were omnipresent in news media coverage. To garner more support outside the university, students set out on a hunger strike in front of the administration buildings, holding another assembly.

As I walked to school one morning, I noticed a crowd of striking students organized at the main campus entrance. The idea occurred to me that I should return home. I felt uneasy. But for some reason, I ignored my instincts and continued on to my first class.

The spacious auditorium was virtually empty. Four, maybe five students. I could hear the gathering storm of protesters through the open windows. Mr. Gottfried greeted me. He was a white American, of German descent, in his late '60s. I had always gotten along with him, and I even thought he had taken a special shining to me. That morning, he called me up to his desk. He wanted to talk about the demonstrating students.

"Mr. Torres. I know I can count on you if they come inside and try to kick us out, right? You will not abandon class, will you?"

I nodded maybe, but I didn't really answer. My stomach lurched up into my throat, and I was quietly hyperventilating as the student group entered the auditorium. They demanded we terminate the class. There would be no studying on their watch. It was a strike. The gaggle was loud and intimidating. Mr. Gottfried cursed the rabbling mass, and he pointed in my direction, ordering me to remain in my seat. The professor clenched his fists, and he looked like he just might be ready to swing at the protesters.

My whole life I engineered my behavior primarily to avoid risk and confrontations. I lived afraid of danger, reluctant to wager my safety for any cause. On that morning, I wasn't especially sympathetic to the protesters—though they had good reason to be upset. If anything, I felt bad for Mr. Gottfried, who had shown an interest in my future. I wanted to prove my loyalty. I wanted to show him I was worthy of his expectations and grateful for his mentorship. But when the other students got up to leave, I couldn't find it within me to stay seated and defend the auditorium with my teacher. I followed them outside, abandoning Mr. Gottfried to the hostile crowd. A dithering lieutenant who was unable to hold the line.

Shame washed over me as I retreated from campus. I recalled being ten years old and seeing my older cousin creeping the bathroom door open to peek at my mom's naked body as she showered. I recalled how I did nothing to stop him. I recalled this same feeling of impotence and cowardice. I felt I was destined to let people down.

I started medical school in the summer of 1982. Sleepless nights, anxiety, and significant defeats and struggles would characterize the next four years. At the beginning of my second year, I was carjacked. It was a terrifying experience for more than one reason.

I had never owned a car in the past. I depended on my dad for transportation while in high school and on public transport in college. When I started dating Elvira, she had her car, and on more than one occasion, she gave me a lift when she was available. As a present for being accepted to medical school, my parents bought me a brand-new car. A 1.8L red Toyota Corolla.

Even though it was my car, my parents made sure that I remembered it belonged to them, and for this reason, they controlled the use of the vehicle. It terrified them I might crash the car and destroy their investment. They wanted to know where I was driving it at all times. I was in medical school!

One night, just before midnight, while driving back from visiting my girlfriend, I got rear-ended on a familiar but desolate dark road. The person in the other car got out and appeared to be hurt.

My medical student instinct told me to get out and provide medical help without it crossing my mind that this could be a trick. Once I approached the other driver and asked him if I hurt him, he pulled a shining silver revolver from his waistband and pushed it against my right temple. He demanded my car keys and my wallet and yanked my beloved chain necklace off me.

He jumped into the driver's side of my car while still pointing the gun towards my face. His first attempt to start the engine was fruitless. Out of frustration, he demanded I get in the car and drive. I knew it would be the end for me if I got inside the vehicle. I found the courage to negotiate with him, and once I started the engine for him, he took off and left me behind in the middle of the road.

I was scared and cried. I began walking until I reached a friend's house, not too far from where I was left. When I knocked on their door, her mom came out and greeted me. I started sobbing and crying. I felt like my manhood had left me.

Then the dreaded moment came. I had to call my parents and inform them I lost the car. My mom's response was what I expected. Her first words were, "I told you not to go out at nighttime!" She uttered this even before asking if I was okay.

They found the car in less than 24 hours—no tires, no engine, no doors. An unbearable feeling of loss and sadness overwhelmed me. The detective who met us at the police station told my parents I was lucky they didn't kill me, which was the way most of these assaults ended. When he asked me to identify the robbers, I panicked. I refused under the pretense I was so scared that I never looked at their faces. This refusal reinforced my low self-esteem and my feeling of cowardice.

Several months later, I checked myself into the emergency room for the first time because of an anxiety attack. It happened in the middle of one of my clinical rotations. From this moment on, irrational fear, anxiety, and panic would characterize my life. My anxiety attacks lasted for ten years until I self-diagnosed my condition and started the uphill battle of finding a resolution to my medical problems.

Irrational fears played an outsize role in my life. I was a medical student during the onset of the AIDS epidemic, and I was always terrified of becoming infected myself.

It was 1984, and I was in my third year of medical school, when I started my clinical rotation at the Medical Center in San Juan, Puerto Rico—the largest teaching hospital on the island. It was the beginning of the AIDS epidemic around the world. We were seeing unusual cases of immunocompromised patients who came to the hospital ill with opportunistic infections never seen in the past.

Just two years later, the CDC reported the first cases of what we now call AIDS in its Morbidity and Mortality Report. In 1983, 14 percent of all incidents reported were among Hispanics/Latinos. It was not until 1984 that Dr. Robert Gallo identified HIV as the cause of AIDS, and a year later, the first test to detect HIV antibodies, Enzyme-Linked Immunosorbent Assay (ELISA), was approved in the US.

During this time, the medical community was ignorant about how the condition was acquired or transmitted. These patients were placed in strict isolation and many times forgotten. Nobody wanted to go inside those marked rooms.

Our superiors used the medical students to do the dirty job of walking into those creepy rooms and performing blood tests, taking body fluids samples. Everybody was afraid of getting the disease from casual contact, including from a simple handshake or a close conversation.

I remember one night when I was assigned to take care of an AIDS patient at the hospital. It terrified me to go inside his room. After donning my disposable gown, a mask, and plastic goggles, I armed myself with sufficient strength to walk inside. I was transported immediately to the hell described by Dante in his Divine Comedy.

The room was dark and only lit by the reflection of the black-and-white TV screen, which was turned on a religious channel where a televangelist was preaching. He was loud and judgmental. He was talking about condemnation from our sins and the fear of hell.

The patient was in his bed, barely breathing, with extreme difficulty swallowing, but not connected to an oxygen tank. He was emaciated and looked ill. My mission that night was to get his arterial blood gases, a procedure that is very difficult to perform even in healthier patients.

As I prepared the needle, my hands were shaking and perspiring. I felt dizzy and thought I would collapse and die in that room. I could hear the preacher from the TV in the background yelling and ordering us to repent before it was too late.

I completed my task and stormed out of that dreadful room. As I was removing my mask, gloves, and disposable head cover, I experienced palpitations, dizziness, and a feeling that I would die.

I never looked back to the bed to say good night to the dying patient. I felt like my fear had dehumanized me, and the only concern in my mind was my survival.

In a way, I behaved no differently than the superstitious doctors in Spain in how they responded to my Tia Lola's cancer. Out of sight and out of mind. Afraid of the unknown.

Many doctors, scientists, and politicians in the 1980s responded to this scary new disease of HIV/AIDS in the same way—by ignoring it as much as possible. This ignorance and lack of research allowed it to spread and kill thousands of people. The uncertainty and social stigma added to the trauma for AIDS patients and their families.

Unfortunately, until quite recently, depression and anxiety have been similarly stigmatized. The human instinct to simply ignore and refuse to talk about anything scary or uncomfortable seems to be widespread.

This stigma is one reason my mother and father never got adequate treatment for their psychiatric illnesses. Although my father was a psychiatrist, he felt that, as a doctor, he was smarter and stronger than his patients. He saw mental illness as a sign of weakness and ridiculed my mother for her own, all the while insisting that his paranoia and delusions were simply objective views of the world.

Imagine how different things might have been if my parents had had proper therapy and medication instead of taking out their fears and anxieties on each other and their children. Imagine how different things might have been if their conditions had not been stigmatized and treatment was widely available. Research into the causes and best treatments of their diseases was a priority for scientists.

We are fortunate to live in the world that we live in today. In most developed countries, disease and illness are no longer treated as scary things to be hidden away and maybe blamed on the people who have them. Instead, they are viewed as part of natural life, and researchers, therapists, and doctors are focused on finding the best ways to help people with these conditions to enjoy life.

But even today, our friends in other parts of the world still face prejudice when it comes to mental illness. Even in the United States, many people feel they don't "need" therapy, or that treatment is "for the weak."

I will always regret how I treated that patient, and I can only hope that my behavior was out of character. Sometimes our fears and anxieties get in the way of our compassion. It wouldn't be the last time I succumbed.

CHAPTER 10

TONY ROBBINS AND POPE JOHN PAUL II

ON OCTOBER 12, 1984, the then-Pope of the Roman Catholic Church, John Paul II, visited Puerto Rico for the first time. My house, like many others, buzzed with anticipation.

For us Catholics, the pope is the successor to Saint Peter, who was himself anointed by Jesus Christ as the head of the church over 2,000 years ago. Saint Pope John Paul II had already visited millions of people around the world, stirring among the faithful a belief in his unique powers of healing and prayer.

My parents were passive Catholics. They were satisfied by attending church on Sundays and talking to the officiating priest at the end of Mass. They never got involved with any church functions or attended daily Mass. They always gave a nominal donation at collection time. They exercised the bare minimum faith they thought required for entry to heaven.

Although they fashioned themselves as religious people, my parents' spirit of sacrifice and giving themselves to the needs of the church was limited. For many years, I too exercised this inherited trait.

I have never volunteered for anything at church or even at school.

Like my parents, I had always given money with no additional commitment which required my physical presence. I am not sure if this was a reflection of our laziness or our fear of commitment.

Over the preceding months, our local church had been preparing us for the pope's visit. My parents had made an unprecedented commitment to be part of this historical event representing our local church. We expected 500,000 people to take part in that day's Mass. To accommodate the large crowds, the government chose to host the Pope in a parking lot. It wasn't just any parking lot. At the time, Plaza Las Americas was the largest shopping mall in the Caribbean, and on a normal Saturday afternoon, the lot was chock-full of cars.

What I remember most about the pope's visit is the connection it forged between me and my parents in the lead-up to and during the event itself. They depended on me to take them to the event, and they felt safe in my presence. We spent the entire day of the pope's visit together and the early evening in a state of joy and happiness, which I seldom experienced before.

We were waiting for the pope's limousine to pass by on its way to the venue. We waited for hours amid a sea of people. Then the black limo appeared, and the crowd erupted. Men and women screamed, trying to attract the pope's attention. We were all hoping he would ask the limo chauffeur to stop the limo and get outside to meet the crowd. I remembered President Kennedy doing the same on that fatal day in Dallas.

I could glimpse the pope briefly inside the car as he blessed us. I felt like he looked at me while making the sign of the cross in the air. I felt like I was in the presence of a saint. This memory has never left my mind and would be critical during times of challenge in my life.

I graduated from medical school in 1986 and they accepted me to a four-year residency in Physical Medicine and Rehabilitation at the local VA Hospital.

The first-year internship was a nightmare. We had to perform at the highest level within the internal medicine department. The head of the department was one of the most feared attending physicians in the entire hospital. His exactitude was legendary. He could make older attending physicians cry at will.

At every morning report, after being on call for 36 hours, I had to confront him and confront my fear of him. More than once, it crossed my mind to quit. However, Mr. Winston's voice inspired me to stay in the fight:" keep kicking, Frisco."

During this first year of medical school I met a man who would change my life. Although he was a peer, he became my mentor.

His name was Francisco, same as mine, but he went by the nickname Paco. He was a few years older than me. He had abandoned the comfort of his home in Asturias, Spain, to move to the United States and pursue a career in medicine. As soon as I met him, I came to admire his determination and his fearlessness. Everyone liked him. He reminded me of my brother, Juan Luis.

Paco had moved to Miami not knowing any English. He had volunteered at the largest local hospital to learn English by wheeling patients around in the emergency room. He had completed medical school in Spain, but he was seeking an American residency in cardiology.

Paco became my role model and the person I aspired to emulate. From the get-go, I wasn't very successful. Paco was gregarious and magnetic. He was self-assured, brilliant.

After his third year of residency, Paco moved to the U.S. to pursue a fellowship. His departure left a deep void in my life. As I was completing my own residency I applied for a fellowship on the mainland too, hoping in some small way to follow him.

I left Puerto Rico on a whim. I saw an advertisement for a fellowship in Louisiana at LSU New Orleans. That was nowhere near Paco, but it felt closer to him.

I already had two small children. My parents and my in-laws were providing child care. My wife had a prestigious job and she was succeeding. I uprooted us based on the fleeting thought this opportunity had to be seized, but also because of my inner desire to follow in my dear friend's footsteps.

I was surprised to get the position. Later, the head of the department told me I was his second choice and that the first had declined the offer. In Louisiana, I faced a new culture, a new language, and the fear of being found out.

My decision to leave the island didn't sit well with my father-in-law, Don José. From the day my wife told him about my intentions, he started encouraging her to change her mind. Don José told my wife she shouldn't give up on her dreams of becoming a great pathologist because Kiko wanted to go to New Orleans in pursuit of a better opportunity to enhance his own professional career.

All her life, my wife had wanted to become a surgeon, but she gave up this ambition for the sake of me and the children. And now, Don José supposed, there would be no opportunity for her to reach her professional goals any time soon. Right before we were ready to board our plane, Don José told my wife to back out. Elvira just giggled it off as if it was a joke. Her response threw him off entirely, and he had no choice but to say goodbye. He loved playing dominos, but Don José had never developed a good poker face. It seemed hard to imagine how he had succeeded in business being as unabashedly expressive as he always is.

After landing in New Orleans, I remember traveling from the airport to meet the program director at the medical center. On the highway leading into the city, I saw a giant and colorful billboard with the words, "Come play golf with us, where the only white thing is the ball."

A feeling of not belonging overwhelmed me again. I had never experienced racial division in my life—at least not that obvious. These words represented to me the struggle of not belonging to either group, black or white.

Within a few months of arriving at LSU, I had to overcome the challenge of conducting medical grand rounds, a major teaching conference attended by well-respected and established attending physicians and professors, including the dean of the medical school. I had to confront my anxieties head-on.

I made slides and wrote and rewrote my presentation. I rehearsed in front of my wife until the words came out. During my performance, I was nervous as I peered out into the audience. I think because my lecture went well, my boss asked me to stay as the director of the electrodiagnostic laboratory.

But that fleeting success did not cure the larger problem. I began experiencing frequent anxiety attacks with unusual symptoms that compelled me to visit the emergency room, complaining of chest pain, and associated dizziness. I convinced myself I was dying. I feared being left alone, and even the thought of driving terrified me. It prevented me from doing the things I loved.

As my attacks increased in frequency and severity, my wife said to me out of frustration: "You had better do something about this…" I heard nothing else. I took it as a threat; she might leave me if I didn't control my condition.

Years later, my wife reminded me she had said if I didn't do something she would take charge of getting me treatment. I wanted to succeed and my drive propelled me past this moment. The incident changed my relationship with my wife and I made poor decisions, which many years later led to a temporary marital separation.

After putting so much effort into my career in Louisiana, I departed on a whim again.

Florida seemed like an opportunity to advance my career, but also to better support my family. I disliked academia at LSU. I landed a new job at a spine clinic in Clearwater under the direction of a colorful cast of doctors. I helped build and develop a local medical business that still employs hundreds of people.

I struggled with my insecurities and fears about financial and professional failure. The bumps along the way convinced me that the only way I have ever overcome my anxieties and panic attacks was to face them head-on.

New to Florida, my anxiety ramped up again. Still, I didn't know what I was facing. This uncertainty created more doubts and sadness.

I continued to counteract the effects of this condition by exposing myself to more challenging situations.

I got into the Tony Robbins philosophy paradigm.

I took part in several of his programs, all of them intimidating. My participation in these was a recipe to trigger a panic attack at any moment in the middle of a 3,000 person crowd. Every time I went through one of his firewalk workshops, which I did over three times, I wanted to run away and never come back.

But something inside of me kept me from quitting. It was the voice of Mr. Winston, encouraging me to "keep kicking, Frisco, keep kicking."

Let me say here that Tony Robbins is a controversial figure in the scientific community. Research doesn't support his claims about the effectiveness of Neurolinguistic Programming (NLP), but millions of followers experience his words and events as life-changing. Research into religious rituals has shown one reason why that might be. Tony Robbins' confidence, enthusiasm, and scary techniques, such as his fire walking ritual, are likely to create a state of high arousal in the brain.[16] In neuroscience speak, that's a state in which many feel-good and reward chemicals, as well as many motivation chemicals, are released. These states *can* help motivate people to act on the principles and ideas in their minds at the time of the experience—but they can also have a dark side.

These high-arousal states can motivate people to do, well, potentially anything. The same language and rituals that can be used to help people ace their presentation for work or undergo a physical fitness transformation can also inspire irresponsible risk-taking and even violence.

Thankfully, most motivational speakers take their responsibilities and the trust of their students seriously. But people have died or suffered from negative consequences as a result of risky behavior induced by an overdose of confidence-and-motivation-enhancing

---

16 Schein, M. (2018, November 28). Tony Robbins Is An Even Bigger Jerk Than You Thought, But You Can Still Learn From Him. *Forbes.*

brain chemicals triggered in self-help courses. In one case where an Australian woman jumped to her death after developing the belief that she could fly during an intense self-help seminar, authorities cited the fact that many self-help gurus are not licensed psychologists, therapists, or psychiatrists. The death caused Australia to reconsider its licensing laws and consider requiring self-help businesses to have licensed counselor or psychologist credentials.[17] Tony Robbins doesn't engage in the most egregious practices, but it's important to keep in mind that to my knowledge he also isn't a licensed therapist or psychologist. For that reason, psychology experts recommend psychotherapy in addition to motivational techniques like Robbins' in order to make lasting changes to relationships and life skills. So although Tony Robbins and oth

So although Tony Robbins and other motivational speakers really *can* help people make positive changes in their lives in the short term, they can also sometimes unwittingly encourage irresponsible or reckless choices. And their practices don't show the same long-lasting clinical effectiveness that's seen with treatment by a qualified therapist.

For me, Tony Robbins' courses helped me achieve several life goals. However, his training also gave me the courage to risk more wantonly, often at the expense of jeopardizing my relationship with my wife and my children. I got the attention of other people at work. I impressed them with external accomplishments and fake confidence. I felt loved and accepted. They admired the fictional person I had created.

The feeling I got from fire walking with Tony Robbins wasn't all that different from what I felt waving back at Pope John Paul II. It was ecstasy. A frantic but evanescent joy. In truth, both oases left me thirsty, because what I needed to do was put in real work on myself. There are no quick fixes for our anxieties and failings. At this time in my life, I still wasn't ready to take responsibility for my future.

---

17   Self-help course led to Australian woman's suicide, sayscoroner. (n.d.). The Guardian. Retrieved from https://www.theguardian.com/world/2009/dec/08/self-help-course-australian-suicide

CHAPTER 11

PANIC AT 2,000 FEET

FOR MANY YEARS I pitied myself over my father's psychological abuse and neglect. Every once in a while, I would undertake dramatic projects in retaliation.

Since I can remember I have been enamored with planes and flying. Back home in Puerto Rico, after I got my driver's license, I used any opportunity to drive to the airport by myself, park, and rush to the observatory to watch the planes take off and land.

I spent hours dreaming about one day becoming a pilot of a large commercial plane. Seeing those gigantic airplanes up close made me feel small, but my dreams soared.

When I turned 16, I convinced my mother to let me take my first introductory flight at a local airport. Against her instincts and her fears of flying, she agreed under one condition—I had to pay for the class. I used all the money I had saved from returning used glass bottles, which I kept hidden under my mattress.

The day I went to the airport with my parents to take my first flying lesson, the sky was crowded with low-hanging grey clouds. I could feel the tension inside the car, and I could see the expression on my mother's face, even without looking at her. She was worried and anxious about where she would hide if a storm appeared. She was smoking her favorite Camel cigarettes, and the smoke inside the car was making me nauseous.

Once we got to the airport, my mother asked me if I had second thoughts. Deep inside, I was torn between my fears and my aspiration to fly. My father answered for me. "You'll see," he said. "Once he gets up in the air, he'll realize he's not cut out to fly airplanes." He said that I was not capable of managing my anxiety, and he insinuated I was not smart enough to handle the controls of an airplane.

He asked my mother with a grin on his face, "Did you bring an extra pair of clean underwear for him?"

We met the instructor, Miguel, at the terminal. He looked about my age, maybe two years older. He reminded me of my brother. My legs shook and a feeling of despair and fear overwhelmed me. Miguel greeted me, and wasting no time, took me straight to the small Cessna waiting for us. I waved at my parents, fearing it was the last time I would see them again.

Inside the plane's cramped cabin, Miguel strapped the seatbelt across my chest, closed the door, and gave me my headset. I experienced a feeling of inner peace. I trusted this young instructor, and I was confident that he would protect me from any harm.

After a quick check ride and getting the clearance from the airport tower, we took off, heading east. After 30 minutes of climbing, we reached our cruising altitude.

It excited me to look through the small passenger window watching the tiny cars driving on the highway. The tall buildings looked like Lego blocks. Once we reached 3,000 feet, we left the thick clouds below and the bright sun appeared, making the skies blue. I saw in front of us a beautiful reddish horizon.

After several minutes of level flying, Miguel asked me if I wanted to fly the plane. Without me knowing, he had already trimmed the plane to keep it steady despite the heavy pressure I might apply to the flying controls.

I could not comprehend how this young man could think I might take control of his small and fragile mechanical bird. Somehow he believed in me, a feeling I didn't experience often. With some initial hesitation and shaky hands, I nodded, and I grabbed the controls. My immediate reaction was to push forward with my hands, strangling the metal handles. At that moment the plane went into a brief nose dive, forcing Miguel to take back the controls.

After he regained control and we had leveled again, he said this with a firm but soft voice, "You have to treat this flying machine like if you were handling a delicate woman." He implied that I had to be gentle, smooth, but firm. He instructed me to keep my eyes on the horizon and not to look at the instruments. After this initial mishap Miguel gave me back the controls.

For the next five minutes, I flew the plane with confidence and relaxation. I believed from that moment on that flying would be my vocation.

"Keep your eyes focused on the horizon," I said to myself.

Once we landed we headed back to the terminal where my parents were waiting with an anxious look on their faces. My heart was full of joy and accomplishment. When we got in the car, the first thing my father said was, "Don't forget that you don't have the 20/20 vision required for airline pilots." I didn't get back into the cockpit of a Cessna for 21 years after that. My father had deflated my ambition.

In Florida, the urge struck me to prove my father he was wrong. I was aimless, struggling to stay afloat. My personal life was in shambles, and I was drowning in my misery. It was the wrong time to decide to fly again.

For several years, my relationship with my wife had been suffering. I was selfish in every way. My own fleeting satisfactions consumed me. I ignored her. I was careless. I could even be cruel. My wife begged me to attend counseling and to change my behavior. I wasn't willing.

I continued to ignore my wife's requests to stop hurting her and the children. I pretended that no issues were affecting us. Outwardly, we performed the loving couple others expected.

It was during this time, after coming back from a weekend in

Fort Lauderdale at one of Tony Robbins' Unleash the Power Within workshops, that I committed to signing up to take flying lessons at a local flying school.

I discovered the toothy giant named Tony one sleepless night in 1991 while I was still living in New Orleans. It was 2 a.m. and I couldn't sleep. I lay splayed out uncomfortably on the family room couch when he first caught my attention. He was 6 foot, 7 inches tall, and he spoke in a husky voice, like my grandfather. He talked faster than I could follow. It was a 30-minute infomercial, playing between 2 a.m. until 5 a.m. every night. By 1991, 100 million Americans had seen the commercials. He had a segment with one of my football heroes, Fran Tarkenton, which caught my attention and lent some credibility to his spiel. Tony was telling Fran how people can achieve whatever they want in life, regardless of their background.

I was vulnerable and felt scared for having moved to the United States with my family, leaving the island and my comfort behind. I was anxious, fearful, and remorseful about abandoning my parents. I was dealing with a terrifying sense of incompetence, both as a man and as a medical doctor.

Tony was a person who had created himself out of the rough material of a rough beginning in life. He was capitalizing on the idea that self-imposed limitations and fears keep us from our dreams.

"You are not a success because you don't want to be one. It's all between your ears," he said. Then he promoted his audio cassettes—Tony Robbins Personal Power: A 30-Day Program. The key to success for a nominal fee of $179.95. There was a 30-day money-back guarantee included. I felt like he was speaking to me and it gave me hope.

After many sleepless nights watching his flashy infomercials, I gave in against my better judgment. I was skeptical of cure-alls and suspicious of ceding $200 during a time in my life when $200 was a lot to give up.

I made the fateful call and ordered the audiocassettes. It was maybe the second or third purchase on my recently approved Visa card, ten percent of my $2,000 credit limit. Little did I know that this sheepish phone call, made alone and in the middle of the night, would change my life forever.

Out of shame, I didn't tell my wife what I had done. I was afraid she would make me return the cassettes. When the tapes arrived at my house, I unwrapped the boxes like when I was a kid opening my Christmas presents. I made a promise to myself to listen to Tony's program for the next 30 days and to do the daily assignments required to qualify for my money back if I chose.

My tendency to procrastinate is undeniable. I have always feared that I was destined not to follow through on my goals. Despite those crippling beliefs and habits, I finished the 30-day program as planned. I felt different, although it may not have been evident to the outside world. I felt confident, and to a degree, more than capable of facing my fears. The program included one section on goal setting. The exercise comprised imagining you own your magical genie who you could ask anything you wanted of, regardless of the outrageousness.

At the end of the exercise, you had to arrange the goals into groups and divide them based on priorities: 12-month goals, five-year goals, ten-year goals, etc. I have to admit that it was a fun drill for me. Today, when I read my original notebook, I can see how far I have come, and most of those dreams are now a reality.

It was on that goal-setting day that I wrote in my notebook one of my most important dreams: to learn how to fly. I had harbored that dream, more or less consciously, since my early student flight in Puerto Rico.

Once we moved to Florida, I frequented a small airport close to my work. I spent hours watching the planes land and take off while getting to know the pilots. The entire experience fascinated me, and I got the urge to fly. However, it was not until a few years later that I got the courage to act on the urge.

One day, while at the airport, I summoned the bravery to ask the front office for information on flying. That day, a young instructor was waiting for his next student pilot to arrive. We struck up a conversation, and in a matter of minutes, I signed up with him and took my first flying lesson that same afternoon.

In those days I was still dealing with my anxiety, although the frequency of my panic attacks had diminished. In the middle of a hectic job and a raucous family life, I continued to drift away from my values—not a good time to focus on learning the fundamentals of flying. However, my ego wouldn't let me rationalize what I was doing, and I continued on my quest to become a pilot.

I was fortunate that my flight instructor, Joel, was a recent graduate from Embry-Riddle Aeronautical University, a prestigious private college in Florida that specializes in training pilots. He was an eager and bright young man trying to accumulate flying hours he needed to earn his commercial pilot's license.

He was very interested in having someone else pay for those hours if he could, so providing lessons was ideal. Instead of making me go through a formal ground school, he decided that it was best for me to fly every time we met. Joel justified his decision by arguing I would learn the theory much faster this way.

That was not a smart choice for my future as a private pilot, but a shrewd move for him to accumulate more hours at a faster rate. I didn't question his wisdom because it suited my love for shortcuts.

It takes the average student pilot between 20 and 30 hours of flying time with a flight instructor before his first solo. In eight months, I logged over 120 hours before my instructor thought I was ready for my first solo flight. In my mind, even after all those hours, I was not prepared. I was afraid of crashing if he left me alone in the cockpit. I feared the worst.

During all my flying lessons, I let Joel handle all the radio communications with the tower. I was afraid of not understanding the air traffic controller or even worse, having to repeat each instruction back to them. This strategy proved to be an almost deadly mistake on the day of my solo.

It was a sultry afternoon in August when Joel decided we should practice touch and go. The airplane cabin was hot, and the air vents spit out lukewarm air. As always, my instructor handled radio communications and I only had to focus on flying the airplane. After the second time around, I felt tired, suffocated by the heat and dizzy. But I said nothing to Joel.

Unexpectedly, on our final approach, he requested a full stop from the tower. It surprised me to hear him say this because we hadn't done a complete regimen of maneuvers, but I was glad we might be finished for the day. After a perfect landing, and before we headed back to the hangar, Joel requested approval for additional touch and go's. When we were going over our routine pre-takeoff safety procedures and before heading towards the runway he turned to me.

"Okay. You are ready," he said. "Today is the big day. Just tell the tower you are a student pilot on his first solo, and they will take care of you."

Before I had time to respond, he opened the door and ran away from the plane. I became paralyzed with fear and hesitation. I had to make a quick decision. Did I return to the terminal, or did I continue in the plane heading towards the runway?

My heart was racing and my palms clammed up with sweat. My chest was tight. I felt like I was drowning. Mr. Wilson's words came to mind like a prayer, "Keep kicking, Frisco. Keep kicking."

The decision was made. I barely had any say in the matter. I contacted the tower and after I identified the airplane with its make and number, I said: "This is a student pilot on his first solo flight requesting clearance for touch and go's."

The air traffic controller replied with a very sarcastic tone of voice, "A student pilot on his first solo? Are you sure you're ready? Remember, this is a hectic airport. There are lots of big airplanes in the air today. You're not allowed to screw up on my watch."

After getting the clearance from the tower for takeoff, I centered the plane in the middle of the runway and pushed in the throttle. The Cessna sped up. Within a few seconds, I was airborne, leaving the airport behind. Suddenly, when I turned my head to the right side looking for traffic and saw the empty seat, I fully realized that my instructor was not with me. I trembled, imagining a crash landing.

I remained in the airport pattern and started the standard procedures for my first touch and go. The air traffic controller gave the clearance to land on runway 17R. He also gave me additional instructions, which I had a hard time understanding.

When the wheels touched the ground, I panicked and forgot to pull back on the throttle to slow down the plane safely. Out of desperation, I slammed my feet on the brakes, making the nose of the plane tip downwards towards the ground.

Just by pure instinct, I could recover and take off without crashing. By now, I was feeling the early symptoms of an impending panic attack. I had a hard time breathing and my neck stiffened, limiting my ability to turn my head towards the left side. I contacted the tower to request a full stop. I didn't declare an emergency or suggest that I was in distress.

I requested clearance for the final landing from the tower. The air traffic controller said something back to me I didn't understand, then the words, "Cleared to land, runway 17." I turned left on my final approach, trying to align the Cessna with the runway.

Suddenly, I heard a scream coming from the radio. It was an air traffic controller. "Do you realize what you just did?! I instructed you to do a 360-degree turn to give time for a 727 to land. You just crossed in front of him! Thank God I gave you both extra space. You could have killed everyone."

On the ground, I headed back to the hangar in a hurry. There, Joel was waiting to congratulate me. I was just happy to be alive. After Joel signed my logbook, I got in my car and raced back to the house. I wanted to tell my wife and kids what I had just done.

When I arrived home, there was nobody. In the kitchen was a note from my wife telling me she couldn't stand it anymore and that she wanted me out of the house. She had taken our children with her and driven to her sister's house in Houston. I tried calling her, but when I spoke to my brother-in-law he said that my wife didn't want to talk.

CHAPTER 12

SEPARATION ANXIETY

THE NEXT TWELVE months turned into a time of intense fear and frequent panic attacks. The separation from my family overwhelmed me with a sense of loss and sadness. I felt I was losing my family and everything I had worked hard to achieve. My behavior had forced me out of the house and confined me to a strange apartment without my wife and children. I feared this was the end of my relationship with my wife, with no point of return. It was one of the darkest moments of my life.

I remember telling my children, "Do nothing if you can't handle the consequences."

Now I had to face the consequences of my actions. Like Abuelo Ramos, I never wanted to feel like a victim. It was as much pride as it was a genuine desire to do the right thing. In any event, here the blame was all mine.

Before my family came back to the house from Houston, I found a one-bedroom apartment a few miles from the house and signed a lease for one year. The apartment was not furnished because I was sure one day I could return to the house. At night, I slept on a cheap mattress on the floor. I purchased a used desk with a plastic chair. In one of my bags, I carried a four-page letter my wife had written to me, describing in detail the pain I had caused her.

Elvira was a kind and unselfish woman who let me visit the children every day so I could continue to be part of their lives. I told no one at work about the separation. The outside world never knew what was going on in my life, although some of them could not help but notice my distraction.

Of all my kids, Daniel was the one who seemed to be affected the most. Every evening after my visit with them, Daniel would ask to come and stay at my apartment. Most of the time my wife indulged him. My son personified the consequences of my behavior. I saw my mistakes in his nervousness and his fear that I would leave and never come back.

Alone in my apartment, a roaring wave of anxiety would overwhelm me. The feeling would pull me under, and I had a drowning sensation like I was dying. When this happened, I would call my wife. More than once, she picked me up and drove me to the emergency room. Mostly, she would calm me down by talking through my attack over the phone.

Six months passed this way. I was isolated from most of my friends. One day I called Paco, who a few years earlier had moved his family to a town in central Florida, near Orlando, just a two hours drive away from where we lived.

I was looking for advice. I wanted to confide in a person I respected and loved. When we spoke, he asked me to come to his house that same weekend. His wife and kids were in Spain, visiting his parents for the summer. He had stayed behind to take care of his medical practice. He regretted having to miss the trip.

"I've never spent a summer away from Asturias since I came over to the U.S.," he told me. "This will be the only time," he swore, more for his benefit.

Paco was close to his family. He knew how much his children enjoyed visiting their grandparents and cousins. You could tell it hurt him to be apart from them.

The weekend was perfect. Paco lived in a spacious house he had designed to fit a one-acre lot in a private, gated community. The yard teemed with trees and flowers. Paco had built a water garden maze around the house and he had filled the aquarium with red and yellow koi fish. He had grown up hiking around his northern Spanish town, which neighbored a national park and the Atlantic Ocean. Unfortunately, his job had afforded him little time outside in recent months. For Paco, the yard and the water garden were a way of keeping grounded.

Paco worked most weekends, so I traveled with him to the hospital on his rounds with patients. The staff loved him. His patients lit up to see him on a Saturday morning. He reached out and shook hands kindly, smiling and joking. But he was methodical, too, and disciplined. After he finished his visits around 1 p.m. we left the hospital to have lunch.

At a diner nearby, Paco was a celebrity. They took us to his favorite booth and asked about his children. Several of the servers stopped off to make sure they could get in a word. I felt like royalty with him.

While we were waiting for our drinks I tried to start a conversation about my situation at home. Before I could say anything, he changed the subject and began asking questions about my work and tennis. In retrospect, I don't think he was interested in condoning my behavior. He preferred to pretend I wasn't that person. Paco was devout. He was pious. He prioritized his wife and children and his patients. He was driven at work by an other-worldly work ethic, and you earned his respect by dignity and honesty.

I felt intimidated and I chose not to discuss my family situation for the rest of the two days we spent together. We played tennis and watched movies on his large-screen television. I left Sunday morning thinking I would get another chance.

A month later, he told me he was seeing a chiropractor because of severe back pain. One week after that he called me on the phone, crying, to tell me they had diagnosed him with terminal pancreatic cancer. The disease had already metastasized widely. I couldn't understand how he could have cancer, and I didn't. What sense does that make? I asked myself.

After Paco's cancer diagnosis, I visited him three times. The last visit was the night he passed away under my watch. Around this time, my panic attacks had continued to escalate. I was afraid of driving myself the two hours to Paco's house. I had to ask my wife to come with me.

The first time I saw Paco after his diagnosis, he was a different man. He looked defeated and sad. He was quiet and withdrawn. The house was busy with people, but they were other people. The kids, who usually clung to their father, didn't understand what was going on. The old positive and happy Paco was gone.

I took Paco with me to run some errands. During that brief trip, I asked Paco how he felt. He confessed to me he felt afraid and a little angry. He regretted having put all his efforts into building a successful medical practice at the expense of his family. He obsessed over the trip to Spain he had missed.

I questioned him about his cancer treatment, but he said, "Kiko, you know as well as I do that I'm dying. There's no cure for this. I'm not going to see my children grow up."

It was the first time in our lives I heard a hint of envy in his voice. To me, it was his way of saying, "Life's not fair. I always did the right thing. I was always thinking of my family, my wife, my church. This is the reward I get?"

"You, on the other hand," I told myself in Paco's voice, "are ignoring God, turning your back on your faith, doing whatever you want… you remain healthy and untouched?"

The next time I visited him, he seemed a little more at peace with himself. He was lying down on the sofa and I sat next to him. On the coffee table was a book on different natural ways to cure cancer. I took a peek. Paco noticed.

"All of that is baloney. There's no cure for metastatic cancer."

All his life, Paco had been a health freak. He was fastidious about what he ate. The few unkind words he ever directed were usually at people who didn't take care of their bodies. Those days I was overweight and out of shape, and I had felt alluded to.

Time passed and I didn't hear from Paco for a while. I didn't have the guts to call him. That would have meant confronting my mortality. One day I mustered the strength to call Vivian, Paco's wife. I asked her how he was doing, afraid of asking for him.

"He's hanging in there, Kiko," she said, tired, her voice longing quietly for something different. "He's at home and we've got nurses. He looks comfortable."

"Do you think I should visit?" I asked her.

The line was piercing silent for what seemed like a minute. "I think you should come," she said.

There was a sense of urgency to how she said it. My heart raced for a minute, thinking about how I would drive myself there. I was still terrified of driving and two hours was a long time for me to be in the car. I can't say what got me there, but I drove, perhaps a little in shock, to see my friend.

I went straight to Paco's bedroom. He lay skeletal and blanched. He could only gasp where words used to flow. The entire house was dripping with exhaustion. His oldest son sat next to his dad, small in a large reclining chair, crying.

I told everyone to go to bed so they could rest. I offered to stay with him that evening. They all went to bed, needing sleep. I stood up close to the bed. I wanted to speak to my friend, but I couldn't say anything. I was afraid. It felt surreal and all too real at the same time.

I wanted to wag my finger at God, but even that useless act felt beyond my reach. I sat down in the recliner. Around four in the morning, I noticed he wasn't breathing. He had passed quietly beside me. I woke the house. We all stood over what was left of his body, sobbing. Even today, if I close my eyes I can still hear his son wailing.

I returned for Paco's funeral. Seeing Vivian and the two boys dressed in black, staring at the casket, brought me back to being a boy and watching President Kennedy's funeral on the television set.

CHAPTER 13

WHERE ARE YOU, GOD?

ALL HER LIFE, my mother was a devoted and practicing Catholic. They raised her in Spain to be a strict adherent to the teachings of Jesus, open-minded to many things, but stern when the situation called for it. Her parents imposed a religious culture in the home, where calendars revolved around a rigid observance of Sunday Mass, Holy Days of Obligation, praying the rosary, and venerating the saints.

True to her upbringing, my mother ensured we went to the best Catholic schools. Despite their modest income, my parents prioritized this education. My mother committed to it as her solemn duty to educate us in the faith. She would often share with me her lingering regret that she had not dedicated her life to God by becoming a nun. I don't think she shared this with many others.

But my mother wasn't all about hard-nosed scriptures. My mother loved to laugh, have fun, and celebrate special occasions. Although she was shy she loved family gatherings, joking around with her children and, later in life, doting on her grandchildren, whom she adored. I especially loved it when she laughed. If you managed to nick her funny bone, she would giggle uncontrollably with tears, convulsing with satisfaction. I delighted in how her laughter melted away all her problems and anxieties, even if just for a moment. In humor, she could shed her fears and revel in the gleeful abandonment of joy.

My mother was an example of service, humility, and love. I saw her deny herself so many times for her children, husband, and parents. She had an incredible sense of duty that, at times, worked to her detriment.

Her life was cut short just before her 70th birthday. One day, like any other, she was helping my sister in the daily cooking and cleaning of their shared home. She slipped on a smattering of water that had been spilled accidentally on the tile floor, and she cracked her hip. She phoned me for help from the floor of the kitchen, writhing in pain. She called me before she called for an ambulance.

I was in Orlando at the time, and I didn't take her pleas as seriously as I should have. I don't recall now what it was I was doing that day, but I am sure it was not important. She begged me to come. She said that she was sure everything would be okay so long as I was by her side. She said she wanted my doctor's touch, but I should have known that what she wanted was her son's embrace. I dismissed her worrying, and I promised half-heartedly to be there as soon as I could. I didn't rush. I made sure an ambulance was on its way.

The ambulance rushed her to the emergency room and I can imagine her gasps of excruciating pain. All those years of slow-building, untreated osteoporosis snuck up on her like a mugger in a dark alley, ready to rip off what is most valuable.

My mother's life changed drastically from that moment on. I knew the thought of becoming incapacitated and depending on others for survival horrified her. After her first surgery, they took her to a local in-patient rehab unit for the next four weeks. She had to adjust and adapt to being told what to do and what not to do. She had to depend on others to get in and out of bed and, to her profound dismay, she required help with her hygiene. She couldn't hide the frustration and hopelessness hardening in her face.

Still, her effort and determination paid dividends. She made quick progress in her rehabilitation. She was counting the days when she could come back home. Unfortunately, her zealousness with exercise resulted in a significant setback. Her hip broke again, and this time it was dislocated. The pain was unbearable. Her lips twisted with agony at the slightest movement. All her hopefulness dissolved in a matter of seconds.

My mother's will was broken. The night before they scheduled her for a transfer to the hospital for a second hip surgery, I stayed with her in a dark and gloomy room at the rehab facility. I never suspected that it was the last night I would spend with her.

I recall the eerie feeling in the air. There was a small color television on the wall in front of my mom's bed. That night the news was talking about Mel Gibson's latest movie, "The Passion of the Christ," a controversial biblical drama. While we were watching this together something happened that caught me by surprise. My mother, a faithful and fervent follower of Jesus Christ all her life, said to me, "All these years of doing the right things to honor and respect God's commands were worthless." This moment was the first time that I had ever heard my mom renounce her Christian beliefs. I answered her more out of instinct than reflection: Mom, this isn't the time to toss your faith aside. This moment is when you're closest to God. She looked at me and didn't say a word. Then she fell asleep.

In the morning, we took her to the hospital for surgery. My brother, whom she loved dearly and deeply, arrived before the surgery from North Carolina. He spent the night with her. Neither of them slept much, and the conversation turned to my mom's spiritual doubts and her fears. They shared a profound conversation where my brother was able to provide her with clarity and comfort. As described by him, she was in total peace and convinced that, whatever came, she was in God's hands when she went in for surgery.

A few hours later, while in her room peacefully recovering, she suddenly developed a severe anxiety attack and she had difficulty breathing. She asked for her anxiety medication. Those were her last words. Moments later she died, at age 69, from an embolism. I looked at her inert body in the bed, where moments earlier she had been speaking with my sister, and I collapsed into myself. I could not prevent this, and, at that moment, all that was unsaid, all that I felt should have done, all the regrets and all the love that we had shared throughout her life shook me with an indescribable force.

I wouldn't be the first person to ask at a time like that why God allows suffering and pain. We've all heard the truisms. God creates a greater good through struggle and unfairness. There can't be light without the contrast of darkness. That didn't help ease my anger and frustration. Within a few years, I had lost my dear friend Paco, and my mother—senselessly before their time.

Eventually, I accepted that we live in ignorance of what lies behind the curtain. The solution I have found to be the most compelling is to surrender to the uncertainty—submit to the Creator, the master planner, trusting that there is a purpose. C. S. Lewis once said, "God whispers to us in our pleasures, speaks in our conscience, but shouts in our pain." It is our limited perspective of universal justice that wicked men should suffer, but good men should be spared. This is, unfortunately, a limited perspective that, from the vantage point of a limitless God, would likely seem naïve. The judgment of people from the sole view of worldly justice is a dangerous enterprise. I think comparing the faults of people is like being at ground level next to two mountains side by side. One is enormous and the other a mere hill. You can tell the difference easily. But if you looked at these mountains from the perspective of great height, even space, the difference between these two mountains would not seem that much. Such is likely God's perspective when weighing the sin of one person against another. No, pain must serve a more long-term, mysterious, and lasting purpose than punishment.

Mental health experts can have mixed feelings about the benefits and risks of organized religions. On one hand, they have shown organized religion as a general category to have strong protective effects against depression and anxiety. People who have a firm view of the emotional and moral order of the universe, and their place and purpose in it, have a significantly better prognosis with mental illnesses of any kind, and even with physical illnesses.[18]

This may be related to the fact that organized religions provide a framework of meaning and value for individuals, their work, and their responsibilities. In studies of mental health in both the clinic and the workplace, a sense of meaning and value placed on one's efforts is associated with better mental health outcomes. In fact, in the corporate world supervisors who practice transformational leadership techniques can improve employees' perception of the meaning and importance of their work and improve their mental health and life satisfaction along with it. The same may very well be true of religious teachers.[19]

Another major benefit of organized religion is likely that of the religious community. Warm, supportive relationships are the principal predictor of a long, happy life, and traditionally, organized religious congregations have been the most common providers of huge support networks of people with meaningful, deep bonds. Both in terms of material and emotional support, the mental health benefits of a healthy, close-knit religious community are unrivaled.[20]

It may also be related to the benefits of the parenting style known as authoritative parenting, in which parents have high expectations and demands of children but also supply high levels of love and support. In healthy religions, where God is viewed as a benevolent parent who wants his children to succeed and treat each other well, religions may serve similar purposes to those of authoritative parents.

Organized religious teachings and communities can also go wrong. For example, some religions and churches can mimic authoritarian parenting styles—where parents demand and expect a great

---

[18] Koenig, H. G. (2012). Religion, Spirituality, and Health: The Research and Clinical Implications. *ISRN Psychiatry*.

[19] Inness, M., Barling, J., & Turner, N. (2008). Transformational leadership and safety performance: The mediating role of meaningful work. *PsycEXTRA Dataset*. doi: 10.1037/e573012012-221

[20] Koenig, H. G. (2012). Religion, Spirituality, and Health: The Research and Clinical Implications. *ISRN Psychiatry*.

deal from children but provide little or no love and support. These parenting styles are associated with poor achievement and mental health among children who experience them.

Authoritative parenting yields the best outcomes among parenting styles, and is associated with promises of rewards for exemplary behavior, encouragement about the child's hard work and achievements, and rules whose logic is clearly explained as benefiting the child and family. These traits of authoritative parenting encourage children to believe that they can achieve great things, reward hard work, and ensure the child they are cared for and protected. By focusing on rules that benefit the child and the family as a whole, the child internalizes the message that following the rules is best for them and others.

Authoritarian parenting, on the other hand, yields poor outcomes. It is characterized by threats of punishment, criticism of the child's performance and abilities, and rules whose logic is centered on serving the parent figure rather than the child. In this model, threats of punishment cause anxiety and fear of taking initiative. Criticism of the child's performance and abilities instill a fear of trying new things and a lack of motivation to put forth the effort. Growing up in a world where rules are centered on serving authority figures and are indifferent to the child's well-being can further enhance a sense of anxiety and insecurity and may create resentment or apathy toward rules and authority figures.[21]

It's easy to see how many organized religions could fall into either category, potentially depending on religious leadership. And we can see how my parents' approach to religion—a severe fear of hell and a punitive attitude toward perceived failings—might have contributed to their anxiety, even as the hope of reward in heaven and belief in God's love for humanity might have soothed it.

Without a doubt, religiosity contributed to my mother's anxieties throughout her life. Equally doubtless, her faith offered great comfort and peace. In her last days, she was battered between the two, but I

---

21 ParentingScience.com. (n.d.). Retrieved from https://www.parentingscience.com/

take happiness from knowing that in her last night on earth she came to terms with the contradiction, while surrounded by her family.

And here we return to the crux of the matter. That is how we respond to pain. I am not trying to minimize the impact of loss and suffering. But I am trying to point to the fact that it is in our ultimate response that we take the potential benefit that brings its purpose. That could be to redefine our course in life, to gain a new appreciation, to understand the fragility of our existence or, ultimately, to make us face the reality that what our soul ultimately is seeking is a relationship with God. That void cannot be filled with anything else. This is the road to healing and restoration for humanity.

My mother journeyed through life weighed down in many ways by the heavy burden of her anxieties. She came to count on medication and prayer to modest yet important positive effects. But it was her relationships with her children and her grandchildren I believe ultimately saved her. Through them, even as she doubted in his will, she was never far from the face of God.

CHAPTER 14

BACK HOME

ONE SUNDAY AFTERNOON in late December, my telephone interrupted the football game I had been watching on TV. The voice on the other end was my wife's, asking me if I was ready to move back home. My apartment lease was about to end, she reminded me. She listed her conditions: I had to change my behavior, attend marriage counseling, and commit to working on our marriage together.

I wavered for a second. This was the invitation I had been anxiously hoping for over the past 12 months, and yet I couldn't answer right away?

In part, my hesitation stemmed from a growing sense that I was starting to figure out my panic attacks. I had become accustomed to my routines, if not happy with them. Thankfully, my hesitation didn't last more than a split second, and I agreed to my wife's terms. I was glad to be going home. And the move back into the house was smoother than what I had predicted. Working on our marriage and rebuilding our family was the priority if I wanted to remain in the house with my children.

A few years later, an invitation arrived in the mail for a medical convention in Hawaii. I thought this was an excellent opportunity to spend some quality with Elvira. It was a five-day trip and I booked two days in San Francisco en route. We both became excited about a stay at Napa Valley, one of our favorite places.

Around that time, I had made an impressive physical transformation and seemed ready to accept the challenge. I also met a local photographer online and arranged for a photo shoot while on the island. I appeared fearless, wanting to put together a 12-month calendar I could distribute to clients, family, and friends.

The bug struck me seemingly out of nowhere. I didn't want to travel to Hawaii and not be able to scuba dive. I had seen photographs of the underwater world—the colors and the alien sea life. I signed up for lessons before our trip.

As I signed up I completely overlooked my debilitating dread of drowning. What about having a panic attack under the ocean, tethered to a breathing tank? I convinced my wife to join me, even though she is not a strong swimmer. I just wanted to take on the adventure as a couple.

After conducting some research online, I signed both of us up for scuba diving lessons at a local dive shop near my work. Our first class was at the store's classroom, which was attached to an indoor swimming pool. That night, another eight people were taking the class. It was a learners' course. I noticed my wife's uneasiness with the class. When the time came to jump in the pool to test our ability to tread water, my wife panicked and fled the premises. I tracked her to the car and asked what was wrong.

She admitted her fear. She didn't want to do it. She seemed unhappy after all the money we had already paid, but she encouraged me to go on by myself. If you had seen us in the parking lot that night, my wife would have seemed afraid, and I would have looked excited. But I was terrified. The water was not my friend either.

I went back to the class without my wife. On our first night, we had to get in the pool with our diving gear, including the massive aluminum air tanks. My anxiety built as soon as I strapped on the tank. My heart was racing and my chest felt tight. At its deepest end, the pool only measured ten feet deep. As I harnessed my air regulator, I noticed my breathing getting faster and shallower. After I mustered the bravery to jump in the water, I felt woozy with an uncanny sense of fear.

At the bottom of the pool, the panic attack set in. I drove up to the surface and yanked the face mask and snorkel from my face, hopping awkwardly onto the side of the pool. I broke down, crying and ready to give up. Then Keith, the diving instructor, sat down beside me.

Keith comforted me. "Do you think I've never had that feeling? Come on. Every one of us has gone through that. The difference between me and somebody who doesn't become a diver is that I just kept on diving anyway. The entire ocean down there is worth it. I promise."

His words gave me the courage to try again.

I didn't know it then, but they consider a history of untreated panic disorders a high risk for diving. Many programs demand you to be cleared by a psychotherapist before they allow you to join. I hadn't warned Keith or anyone else about my condition.

Once in the water, Mr. Wilson's words came to my mind, "Keep kicking Frisco, Keep Kicking…" I finished my assignment for that session and I kept coming back for more classes. I finished the certification just in time for our trip to Hawaii. Like I invariably do, I took shortcuts while learning the theory, another crucial mistake that I would regret on subsequent dives.

We landed in Maui; the island chosen for the medical convention. As soon as we dropped off our bags at the hotel, I went straight to the diving shop to inquire about a basic diving day trip. Unfortunately, all the level one trips were sold out. I was disappointed that all the time and effort certifying would be for naught.

Suddenly a man emerged from the back office—physically robust, towering, and tanned. He presented himself as the shop's divemaster. He had heard my conversation with the attendant, and he came to suggest an option.

The first question he asked me, with a deliberate tone of voice was, "How many dives have you done?"

The question caught me by surprise, but I answered, "More than five."

"I have a challenging trip coming up tomorrow," he told me, "but it's only for someone who can handle tight spaces and who will not panic."

My palms clammed up and yet I said, "I'm your man."

He followed up with another question about how deep I had reached on my past trips.

"90 feet," I replied.

In truth, I had only done one open ocean dive, and it was just 40 feet.

That night I couldn't sleep. I was nervous and concerned about what I had signed up for. After a few hours of sleep, I woke up early in the morning and felt an impending sense of doom and uneasiness. However, I picked up my diving equipment and headed toward the dive shop. I found Tony, the divemaster, at the front office. I couldn't believe it when he said, "Okay, Francisco, it's only you and me. The other two guys chickened out."

I felt like running and never looking back. However, Mr. Winston's words and Keith's encouragement kept me put. Tony began the brief about our diving trip. It was a shipwreck located 80 feet underwater, about a mile and a half from the coast.

He was planning to go inside the ship and into a cabin with an air pocket formed by the air from previous divers, where we would remove our masks and air regulators to make our dive last over 55 minutes. He was also planning on using underwater electric scooters to preserve air, allowing us to make it back to the beach.

Once we reached the shipwreck, I hyperventilated. I focused on sea life. My fears evaporated as I dove further. The inside of the ship filled me with awe. We came into a tiny chamber with space barely wide enough for the two of us. I was glad I had been watching my figure. The crucial juncture came when the master diver told me to go above water and put my head in an air pocket.

We were 80 feet below the surface. Once inside the bubble, he asked me to remove my face mask and the air regulator. I had to depend on him to make it out alive. Once I did it I felt like someone had detached a heavy burden off my chest. The feeling of drowning was no longer overpowering me. It was the first time in my life I felt I had achieved something of significance.

We headed back to the sand, and once we arrived, Tony said to me, "You're a brave dude. You don't realize how many divers have turned around and given up just before entering that chamber. Divers with years of experience."

CHAPTER 15

THERAPY

MY LIFE STARTED to turn around. But I didn't deal with my anxiety alone. For many years I avoided professional help. My father had always denigrated psychotherapy. He warned my mother against revealing too much to doctors who could use her words against her. He—a practicing psychiatrist—claimed that therapists might brainwash their patients, implanting unwanted thoughts through hypnosis or subliminal suggestions. It was difficult for me to accept my mental health problems were actual health problems and not just a defect of character. My marital strife had changed my attitudes, and my wife convinced me to finally seek help.

Unfortunately, my first experience seeking out a therapist wasn't successful. After talking to a psychiatrist friend informally about my emotional situation, he recommended that I see a local psychologist. Even though I didn't think I was mentally ready, I made an appointment.

It was a rocky start. On my first visit with the psychologist, I immediately sensed a lack of empathy and emotional distance. I felt judged and disliked by him. I initially opened myself up and warned him about my tendency not to follow through on many of the things

I embark on, including trying to take care of my mental health. It didn't take long for him to use this against me. After several visits, I told him I had to reschedule some of our sessions due to work obligations. Without hesitation, he told me I was again sabotaging my treatment and mentioned I was mentally weak and unable to commit to my psychological well-being. Suddenly I saw the figure of my father, judging with a look of dislike in his eyes. I never went back to the therapist's office.

Fortunately, I didn't give up on the desire to find the right therapist who could set me in the right direction. Many years passed until one day at work while talking to a nurse, Mary, she mentioned she had become a certified psychologist with a subspecialty in anxiety, post-traumatic stress disorder, and panic attacks. She had opened an office and was working part-time, hoping to leave nursing and become a full-time psychologist. I already had a great rapport with her and enjoyed our frequent conversations while professionally interacting at work. The thing I liked the most about her was she was not judgmental and she didn't feel threatened by a medical doctor. She also believed in bibliotherapy as a valuable part of psychological healing. The fact I felt more comfortable talking to a woman may have played a role in my decision too.

After two years of regular visits and follow-through on the reading assignments, I have to admit it was the first time in my life I felt I was discovering myself and taking control of my actions and destiny. In one of our first sessions, Mary introduced an innovative and non-traditional type of Cognitive-Behavioral Therapy (CBT) called Eye Movement Desensitization and Reprocessing (EMDR). CBT and EMDR have been equally valid forms of treatment for anxiety and stress disorders. EMDR is specifically targeted to treat Post-Traumatic Stress Disorder, which Mary thought was the origin of my anxiety and panic disorder.

I remember our first session. She provided me an electronic tablet with a pair of headphones connected on one side and invited me to sit on a very comfortable sofa. She sat in front of me, holding an erasable whiteboard with sentences on it. She dimmed the lights and turned on the tablet. To my surprise, it was just a blank screen with a red ball bouncing from one end to the other. She connected the tablet to a speaker, and every time it jumped it made a loud electrical sound.

She then explained she would ask me some questions about my childhood and for me just to concentrate on the ball bouncing from side to side while it was making the sound. Before starting the test, I had to focus on a negative or emotional thought associated with a specific memory or image. After a minute she turned off the tablet and asked me to let my mind go blank and to notice the thoughts and feelings I was having spontaneously. After a while, the initial distress over a particular thought, memory, or image faded. Although this therapy proved beneficial in the long run, I have to admit it was emotionally stressful while moving through the treatment. What I valued the most was it didn't rely on talk therapy or medications.

I clearly remember one emotionally charged session. While concentrating on a specific memory, suddenly the figure of Joe 90 appeared in front of me. When I was nine years old, I had a dream about who I wanted to be. Joe 90 was a British science-fiction television series that portrayed the adventures of a nine-year-old schoolboy, Joe McClain. Joe becomes a spy after his dad creates a device capable of recording expert knowledge and experience which he could transfer to another human brain. Armed with skills from the world's top academic and military minds, Joe became an agent for the World Intelligence Network (WIN) and they named him its "Most Special Agent." The show used marionettes of natural body proportions. Joe was the same age I was and it made my imagination soar. They set the series in the future, possibly an undetermined year in the 21st century. To the outside world, it was just an ordinary father-and-son relationship.

However, there was a secret laboratory in the house's basement, which had Professor McClain's latest invention, the Brain Impulse Galvanoscope Record and Transfer machine—"BIG RAT." The heart of the BIG RAT was the "RAT TRAP," a spherical cage in which

Joe sat to receive the recorded brain patterns. While wearing special glasses storing the brain patterns, he could undertake assignments, including piloting a MIG jet, performing neurosurgery, or playing the piano.

After watching an episode, as soon as I was in my bed at night, I started dreaming of being Joe 90. I wanted to be loved by my dad while working together on different exciting missions, trying to save the world from threats of nuclear war. I wanted to gain all the knowledge possible without studying or going to school. I wanted to spend time with my dad and make him proud of me. Those dreams at night kept me company in those beautiful days when there was not much money for toys. Immediately a sense of sadness invaded my dream, reminding me I could never achieve the relationship with my dad I desired so much.

As with all types of medical or health treatment, the clinical discipline of psychotherapy is based on decades of experimental evidence about how best to conduct relationships and have a sense of well-being. Therapists don't just make guesses or operate based on unsubstantiated therapies. They study decades of experimental research to learn what works best.

And studies show that having someone in our lives who has this knowledge and can use it to guide us regularly can undo the damage of years or even decades of abuse. Though our brains and our epigenetics can be scarred by childhood abuse, we can undo these changes with the right influences from a good therapist. Studies of PTSD in veterans have shown that psychotherapy, including EMBT and EMDR, can change the activation of a gene associated with vulnerability to stress. The gene whose expression changed as a result of therapy is a gene associated with the ability to handle stressful events without experiencing overwhelming, painful emotions.[22] Part of psychotherapy realizes that other people may not have as much power over you as

---

22   Can Psychotherapy Reverse Post-Traumatic Epigenetic Changes? (2019, October 29). Retrieved May 22, 2020, from https://www.psychologytoday.com/us/blog/psychiatry-the-people/201910/can-psychotherapy-reverse-post-traumatic-epigenetic-changes

you once thought. As much as I wanted a relationship with my dad, I eventually realized that my life was better when I wasn't trying to please him or win his approval. Many of us encounter similar dynamics in our lives—we want someone's love or approval, but trying to win it makes our lives worse.

Eye Movement Desensitization and Reprocessing therapy work based on the concept that past trauma continues to affect us if we do not process it healthily. As we discussed in the earlier section about healthy grieving, painful emotions often can't be processed or healed until we experience them vividly and openly.

Sometimes our natural response to painful events—like my father's rejecting behaviors toward me—is to pretend that they are not happening or that they do not bother us. That creates neural networks in the brain that shape our thoughts and behavior for a long time to come, but we may not even be aware that they exist. We may think of the way we behave and think as "just the way things are" and not realize there are other options.

EMDR uses neuroscience techniques to help us access those old, painful memories. It hurts to be reminded of them, but by experiencing that pain within the neurological activation produced by the therapy, our brains can process those emotions and create new patterns around them. By experiencing these painful feelings and events with the help of Mary, a supportive and qualified person who I trusted, I was able to re-form many of my thoughts and feelings about myself. As a result, I could become more secure and loving in my relationship with my family.

I no longer feared that my wife would leave me if I were too "weak." I no longer felt that I had to do exciting—and maybe dangerous!—things to prove my worth. Instead, I was able to appreciate the family and career I had created.

My family and career were impressive by anyone's standards, but I had long been unable to feel that way because I had so often received the message early in life that I would achieve nothing and never be good enough. Through therapy, I was able to change the patterns these messages created deep within my brain and DNA. As a result, I became happier and less anxious.

In this way, therapeutic progress can sometimes be made even faster and more powerfully than through traditional psychotherapy based on talking about your problems. After all, we can still deny to ourselves that problems exist or that they bother us even while talking about them. EMDR, however, affects the neurons of the brain in a specific way to bring these harrowing experiences to the surface and take away their hidden power to influence us. When we access these memories in EMDR therapy, our conscious, healthy skills and beliefs can rewire our minds and behaviors based on old events and suppressed feelings.[23]

EMDR isn't the only kind of psychotherapy that's shown to be highly effective or to produce epigenetic changes. Cognitive-Behavioral Therapy and Dialectical-Behavioral Therapy have also been scientifically proven to produce epigenetic changes along with significant improvements in the well-being, confidence, and emotional distress of patients.

According to the Anxiety and Depression Association of America, another type of therapy, called Interpersonal Therapy, has been shown to produce significant improvements in depression but has not been studied for epigenetic effects yet.[24]

Therapy complemented the coping mechanisms I had developed on my own. I'm confident I wouldn't have achieved genuine success without it.

---

23   What is EMDR?: EMDR Institute – EYE MOVEMENT DESENSITIZATION AND REPROCESSING THERAPY. (n.d.). Retrieved May 22, 2020, from https://www.emdr.com/what-is-emdr/

24   Psychotherapy Approaches: Which Have the Most Evidence of Success? (n.d.). Retrieved May 22, 2020, from https://health.usnews.com/health-care/patient-advice/articles/2017-06-30/psychotherapy-approaches-which-have-the-most-evidence-of-success

CHAPTER 16

CERTAIN ABOUT UNCERTAINTY: PANIC FOR THE NEW MILLENNIUM

ON JANUARY 18, 1999, Time Magazine ran a front cover proclaiming "The End of the World!?!" This sensationalist headline triggered a wave of concerns over the coming year 2000, the new millennium. After its publication, several cultural figures, including religious and political leaders, exploited this opportunity to predict airplanes falling out of the sky, computers on the fritz, a ruptured economy, malfunctioning nuclear missile systems, and the impending collapse of society as we knew it.

On March 31, 1961, a few months before my first birthday, a Time Magazine cover featuring an image of Edvard Munch's "The Scream" pronounced that the era of the sixties was "almost universally regarded as the Age of Anxiety." It was like I had been fated to suffer this same disease. The dread of a nuclear war between the United States and Russia was a legitimate menace in the world. It captured the attention of millions, including my family. I recall the drills at school preparing us for a nuclear strike. Any time I went out with my parents we were continually scouting for the symbols marking the secure places to hide in case the Russian's decided to strike.

In the initial months of 1999, I recall reading on the internet about a Christian economist named Gary North. Mr. North warned of doomsday and an inevitable calamity in the coming days. To prepare for a "Post-Y2K Anarchy" he called for the U.S. government to return to Old Testament Law. Because of his many apocalyptic prophecies, he received the nickname, "Scary Gary." He wasn't the only one spreading fear.

"Survivalists" became a frequent topic of debate in the media. The survivalists were people who, daunted by the prospect of a universal computer-generated disaster, stocked up on groceries and other supplies. Like-minded doomsday believers started banding together. It was a whole movement, sharing MacGyver-esque tips and hairbrained strategies for saving yourself. Unfortunately, some of these folks turned to violent defenses of the precious supplies. They rapidly captured our imagination, becoming "the prophets of doom."

By the start of that same year, 1999, I had diagnosed myself with an anxiety disorder characterized by panic attacks. I was determined not to use medications in controlling the disease. However, as I noted earlier, my initial attempt to seek relief with psychotherapy was unsuccessful.

The hysteria repeatedly displayed in the media during this time fueled my anxiety and fear. I started devouring books on anxiety and panic attacks. I turned to bibliotherapy as a method for managing my psychological ills. I, too, elected to confront my fears head-on by relying on my inner strength. I became, in my mental world, a survivalist.

The first six months of 1999 were also stressful at the office. After a string of poor business decisions combined with an increased need for capital in the run-up to 2000, the prospect of bankruptcy became a real menace. The threat overwhelmed me with uncertainty about our future. On the horizon, I worried my fears of ineptitude as a provider for my family might be confirmed.

My earliest childhood fears of losing our house were materialized again, bloating my anxieties. By the summer of that year, economic matters settled down at work, and it was the first time we saw a brighter future in front of us despite what was going on around the world. We employed a new CEO who would eventually reverse our financial position in a matter of months.

That summer I pledged to transform my body into the lead-up to my fortieth birthday in September. Growing up, I always looked at magazines with pictures of fit men displaying tan six-packs. Like many, I ascribed that level of genuine success to rare human gifts. But for whatever reason, that summer, I decided to take control of my appearance.

I used my journal writing as a way to hope and plan, but also to bring about my goals. The first task I undertook after writing those goals and setting up a 90-day health and fitness program was to sign up for a gym membership. I have to admit that my path wasn't straight or smooth. It was rugged and winding, and I couldn't always see the finish line.

When I first set foot in the gym, I wasn't sure I could get started. My quest began with a feeling. It was a feeling that by taking care of my body, my psychological health would follow. That feeling gradually turned into a desire and a passion, not only to exercise but a wish to celebrate my body in a manner I had only ever seen others do.

I knew the basics. I read many textbooks on exercise and nutrition. I got to where I could run several short distance races, and I dropped a lot of the weight I had always longed to lose. But my fear and my insecurity held me back. I kept involuntarily reminding myself that I would never be and never had been a gifted athlete.

I didn't even like the gym, I would say to myself. I was terrified and anxious about plunging into an environment where everybody seemed to know more about what they were doing than I did. And they all seemed to be so much farther along the road than I was.

That's where my first health and lifestyle coach, Doug, made all the difference. When I met him he was in his late teens. He was young, fit, and handsome. He always had a new girl waiting for him at the end of our sessions. I started wishing I could look like him, even though I was 20 years older.

Doug took the raw feeling I had when I first began this journey and turned it into a work ethic, a passion, a commitment, a triumph. If I hadn't taken the initial step of hiring him, I could never have achieved what I did. I wouldn't have even recognized what was possible.

Like so many of us who struggle with our physical appearance, I had low self-esteem. I could force myself to write in my journal I would achieve a six-pack, or close my eyes and visualize a chiseled future, but I never really believed it. I thought the genes didn't add up. Doug changed that for me by focusing on concrete, small steps I could take. It worked.

However, while I went through a dramatic personal transformation, life around me didn't change at the same pace. I had to face the same everyday struggles and challenges. The only difference was that I was more attentive to the material things I wanted to get and acted more confidently. My life needed to change in the long term.

I became a casualty of my own exaggerated pride. I needed another weapon in the fight against self-doubt and despair. I started compensating for my low self-esteem with the addition of "things." I created a fictitious external world which covered up my vulnerabilities and fear of the unknown. As the end of the 20th century was approaching, my only worry was to have the desired physique to reveal to whoever would see my pictures.

I believed then that the new body with the six-pack washboard abs would make me more appreciated and accepted. I was desperately seeking validation from others. I didn't care whether the chaos all these religious individuals were predicting was any part of God's design. I was not interested in having a contingency plan for Armageddon.

The constant fluctuation between extraordinary triumphs and demoralizing failures marked the next decade of my life. All the physical gains I made after two years were gone. During that time, external successes cast a shadow over an internal feeling of self-doubt, anxiety, and fear. Again, my family paid the cost of my emotional instability.

I clung to my Tony Robbins routines. He promulgated quick fixes to chronic issues, downplaying the effectiveness of years of conventional psychotherapy. As I have mentioned before, he promoted a technique called Neurolinguistic Programming (NLP). This approach, coupled with my negative experience with psychiatrists and psychologists, pleased me.

I continued to investigate the roots of my internal turmoil. To the outside, however, I put on a smile. My spiritual life was non-existent, and for me, God had grown silent. But in the quiet places, I knew that a heavy sense of guilt had been fueling my anxieties since I was a child.

Tony Robbins taught me the world was mine to create. This philosophy conflicted with my philosophy on life. I had always been told by my family, priests, and Catholic teachers that everybody was born with the consequences of original sin and that guilt was part of human nature. Our imperfections as human beings compound this guilt. According to them, the only remedy is our faith and compliance with the rigid implementation of the Ten Commandments, as well as the Church's teachings and doctrines.

Once I replaced the original sin concept with Tony Robbins' teachings my faith in a higher entity diminished, and I shifted the focus to me and my decisions. I became God. I felt alone in an empty universe and answerable only to myself. I went from the fear of hell to the fear of insignificance. For a long time, this way of reasoning seemed to be a satisfactory replacement for my Catholic faith, and I continued to make significant external progress.

However, many years afterward it became clear that a belief only in myself could not provide what I desperately needed—self-acceptance and purpose. During the next few years, I devoted most of my time thinking only about myself. Later in life, I realized, guilt can be a well of selfishness.

To the external world, I portrayed an attitude of caring and love toward my fellow man, but on a personal level, I had a hard time tolerating the needs of others. Having feelings of guilt doesn't give you a clear moral code. Disordered guilt is often born of narcissism, and both will lead to anxiety.

I witnessed this with my father, who always outwardly expressed his guilt about making erroneous decisions and harming people. He would declare himself as a "grand criminal." For this reason, he had to go to confession every time he visited the church. But his behavior was contrary to his words. He could communicate his guilt to the world while at the same time he could be cruel and mean to his wife and children, but never to strangers. It was like he was using guilt as self-validation for all the shameful things he had imposed on his family along the way. My dad always thought he could redeem his guilt by handing out money or presents to others, with no other effort.

Every time I ponder the notion of original sin and collective guilt, I feel responsible for something I didn't do. I grew up with a Catholic faith which proclaims we are all imperfect from birth. This way of thinking filled me with doubt about myself and planted questions about my beliefs as I grew up. I imagined heaven or paradise as a place without guilt. The day I left Puerto Rico and moved to the United States, my parents made sure that I felt the guilt of leaving them behind and I never felt forgiven by them, no matter what I did.

Now, at this stage of my life, I know you can't make someone feel guilty. It has to come from inside the individual and his emotions. That is why my brother, Juan, never felt guilty for leaving the house when he was in his early 20s. He was tougher than me, both emotionally and psychologically.

Guilt, for the emotional and vulnerable individual, is difficult to shake off. The minute you decide to bury it, suddenly it sinks its tentacles inside you even harder. To this day, I still bear with me the guilt about my parents, even when I moved both of them to Florida to be closer to the children and me. It never was enough for them, and they never expressed a genuine feeling of appreciation.

Although guilt can be deemed a neurosis as well as a selfish trap, it can also be a positive drive when appropriately managed. Both psychologists and theologians agree a certain measure of guilt and anxiety is needed in a person. Like with pain, reasonable quantities of guilt are vital for survival. Not only does it warn you of imminent danger, but it also makes you responsible for other human beings.

We are all familiar with the television villain—a classic serial murderer who demonstrates no remorse. He lacks a sense of guilt. We relate them with monsters and immorality. But the sociopath has something on us mere mortals. The lack of guilt means a lack of anxiety. Ever notice they're never afraid of getting caught? At present, research cannot prove a definitive link between guilt and anxiety, but in many ways, we can seek a connection with our own two eyes. But there is a difference.

Guilt is an uneasiness over something wrong committed in the past, either real or imagined, while anxiety typically involves possibilities that can happen in the near future. Some neuroses we observe in most mental conditions are a defense mechanism against anxiety. Phobias are an attempt by our psyche to repress anxiety and guilt, which is too painful to accept. The individual develops an irrational aversion to a situation unconnected with their fear.

Psychologist Rollo May defined anxiety as the fear of losing a mother's love, and hence, self-esteem. Later on, Otto Rank, Freud's disciple, talked about the concept of birth trauma. To him, life was a process associated with a series of separations, starting at birth. He correlated anxiety with the apprehension involved in these separations.

Professor Henry Stack Sullivan made the argument that anxiety arises from the infant's apprehension of disapproval. Change, besides separation, also becomes a threat, and threat produces anxiety.

America, my newly adopted country, promoted this axiom: the individual, regardless of his background or social situation, can accomplish anything if he tries hard enough. This mentality turned, possibly, into a primary cause of my anxiety. It always reminded me to ignore my limitations, but more than that, to defy them.

This made me more aware of my lack of significant talents, or of not being intelligent enough to reach the goal. After I turned 40, growing old became my number one concern. This obsession inspired me to research anti-aging medicine and eventually to get certified and become a patient in the same field.

In the beginning, this was an interest in the health benefits of exercise and a well-balanced diet. Later it became an urge to cheat aging by using hormones and supplements of dubious scientific validity. I turned into the gym rat I never thought I would be and created my company around pictures of me with exercise videos.

I found the "Fountain of Youth" and became an "expert" on anti-aging medicine. I based my life during that time on external status symbols, such as a fancy wardrobe, a luxury home, and souped-up automobiles.

In 2010, I wanted to expiate my inherited guilt by doing something for the common good. I tried to use altruism to redeem myself from all these excesses and selfishness. When I learned in early January about the devastating earthquake that hit Haiti I committed to going there as a medical volunteer, even though I had no experience volunteering like that before.

CHAPTER 17

EARTHQUAKE

ON JANUARY 12, 2010, at 4:53 p.m., two tectonic plates 15 miles southwest of Port-au-Prince, the capital of Haiti, suddenly slipped. The dormant fault had fractured the earth, rumbling potently through the island. The unprecedented 7.0 magnitude earthquake inexorably shattered the entire capital city. The shaking lasted only 30 seconds, but for that country, those 30 seconds were an eternity with devastating consequences.[25]

The earthquake demolished the Presidential Palace, a three-story concrete building. Rene Preval, the president, was missing. People dreaded the worst. Fortunately, he was not in the building when the earthquake struck. But he remained in hiding, assessing the horror silently before speaking to the nation.

Word of the tragedy spread like wildfire across the world. The international community heard the cry for help and they answered. This was an unprecedented magnitude of human suffering and need. The barrage of daily news drew attention to the overwhelming situation, and I felt drawn to do something. After all, it was the most

---

25 Haiti: Ten years after the earthquake. (n.d.). Retrieved October 15, 2020, from https://www.doctorswithoutborders.org/haiti-ten-years-after-earthquake

devastating natural disaster of the 21st century. I had to do more than write a check. I felt a powerful desire to become involved.

Naturally, I was intimidated and hesitant about what to do. It's one thing to hope you can help. It's another thing to actually do it.

I called Scott, one of our staff orthopedic surgeons, because he had experience volunteering during international disasters. I asked him to consider me if he got involved with a humanitarian medical mission to Haiti. At first, he was skeptical. He asked me, "Do you want to go? You know what you're signing up for?"

The reality was that I am a pain management physician. I'm not a surgeon or an internist. The situation in Haiti was precarious, even dangerous. The supply of medication was dwindling as the need spiked and they desperately needed generalists. "We can make it there in the next few days," Scott said. "But we won't have a return ticket. Are you sure you want to do it?" I hesitated, and my voice cracked a little. "I'm sure. Count me in," I answered.

I didn't hear from Scott for a few days. Every time my phone rang, I panicked, overwhelmed with butterflies. I kept watching the coverage on the news. The images were shocking—a mass graveyard of cement. Sometimes in the wreckage's video sounds could almost be heard, seemingly of muffled cries for help beneath the rubble. Before the earthquake, Haiti was already in dire economic and societal straits. Haitians were suffering from severe limitations in infrastructure and had anemic economic prospects. Haiti was the poorest country in the Western Hemisphere. To aggravate matters, the AIDS epidemic from the 70s and 80s had strained the health care system.

I needed to position my life and mental state, leading to my decision to become involved in helping with this tragedy. Over the past several years I had conditioned my body through exercise, diet, and new healthy habits. I was in the best shape of my life. In 2008, after completing a challenging and grueling certification in anti-aging medicine, I opened my own business, Forever Young, MD. I became the poster boy for the business and I used my before and after pictures to advertise the product. I built a medical company promising a fountain of youth. I exploited the human desire for immortality.

I focused the entire business on myself and what I considered incredible achievements. I even commissioned a local artist to paint a portrait of me with my shirt off, exposing my chiseled body and my six-pack abs. I hung the oil painting in my office for everyone to see. I sought fiercely after the antidote to my sense of insignificance and insecurity. So, naturally leading up to the trip to Haiti, I focused heavily on training my body. I did not suspect that I was neglecting what would come to matter most.

I was very confident in my physical condition, and I recognized the mission would be extremely physically demanding. If I am honest with myself, I wanted to show others I was brave. Truthfully, I was seeking recognition and admiration. Subconsciously, I must have felt my participation in this effort might even help my new business to take off. I wanted to be known as a hero! My ego got me to Haiti.

One Friday evening I received the dreaded call from Scott. He was all business. "Francisco, it's a go! My buddy has a Learjet he can donate. It's waiting at the airport for us, and we can take it to Fort Lauderdale."

From Fort Lauderdale we had to find our own flight to Haiti. We were meeting another orthopedic group to join forces. The plan was to transport considerable medical and first aid supplies. Scott had organized donations from several local hospitals.

As soon as I hung up with Scott, I turned to my wife, who was sitting next to me, and I asked her what I should do. I was hoping she would beg me not to go. To my surprise and chagrin, she was supportive. She encouraged me to seize the opportunity to help others. She started helping me pack right away. For me, it was another sleepless night. My wife and I had talked about the diseases I might encounter—cholera, malaria, salmonella. That night I had to find a 24-hour drugstore to buy a supply of antibiotics and antidiarrheal medications.

The next morning my wife drove me to the local private airport, where I was meeting the rest of the crew. Watching my wife drive away, a sense of loneliness overwhelmed me, abandonment even. It was as if my parents were leaving me at swim class all over again. I feared I might just drown in my anxiety.

The airport staff and the crew of the plane were warm and appreciative. They treated us as if we were courageous and caring for what we set out to do. At least at that moment, I felt the admiration I was looking for. The flight to Fort Lauderdale was brief, comfortable, and uneventful. They stocked the plane with food and alcohol, which helped me forget for a moment where we were headed. We met the rest of our team in Fort Lauderdale. They were already searching out a plane to take us to Haiti.

Dusk came, and it got dark quickly. While we waited, I considered renting a car to drive back home to Tampa. I could use the difficulty of finding a plane as my excuse. Scott was too resourceful to let that happen. He struck up a conversation with a woman waiting at the private airport with her children. Her family was on its way to take them to the Bahamas for a holiday trip. Scott didn't have to sell it very hard. As soon as she heard what we needed, she directed her private Lear Jet crew to take us to Haiti that very night. She volunteered to stay the night in Fort Lauderdale with her kids, deferring their vacation.

She humbled me with her decisive act of charity. I mustered a little bit of my confidence back and braced myself for the journey. I didn't recognize this at the time, but her generosity prompted a new resolve in me. I started to seek out the greater purpose.

We began loading the plane. We could barely meet the FAA weight guidelines for safety. We loaded supplies everywhere they fit, including into the cramped lavatory. We all had to agree not to use the toilet in flight. All of us were afraid of leaving some lifesaving supplies behind. The mission was too critical.

At that moment, Roberto Clemente came to mind. I remembered flying almost 40 years earlier over the Coast Guard units who were searching desperately in the waters off the Puerto Rican coast for Clemente's plane. I remember how sad I felt at the loss of two heroes—the baseball player, and my grandfather, who lay back on his deathbed in Spain.

Clemente had died on a humanitarian flight to Nicaragua. He had likewise loaded his plane with supplies. A few minutes after takeoff, his plane had crashed due in part to the excessive weight of the load. On his mission, Clemente wanted to be certain he was taking as much as he could with him to help the people of earthquake-stricken Nicaragua. He wasn't thinking about his own personal safety. This made me reflect. What was I truly scared of? Was it not having enough supplies for the victims of the quake? Or was it my own safety? Was my charity pure, or was I motivated entirely by self-interest? The thought made me feel ashamed.

We landed the plane in Port-au-Prince. I stepped out onto the makeshift tarmac managed by American military troops. Unloading was easier than cramming everything in. I noticed tons of supplies unattended on one of the airport terminals. I wondered why those supplies had not been handed over to the people in need. I was also suspicious about the fact that they had been there for so long. This made us very watchful of our supplies. We didn't know where we were going or where to stay. Out of sheer luck, a group of retired American military personnel, including a group of doctors called Team Rubicon, asked us to join them for the rest of their mission. They assumed we were a group of medical professionals they had been waiting for. As it turned out, the group never showed up and, instead, we took their place.

We packed our supplies into a pickup truck, guarded by one of the Rubicon team members, and we headed to our quarters. None of us knew where we were going with no notion of our ultimate destination. The air was damp and ominous, and the stench of decomposing corpses nearly bowled me over. We arrived at a large compound that somehow had remained visibly unscathed by the quake, and we entered through an immense steel gate. At that late hour, just past midnight, there was an enormous crowd of people standing at the entrance wanting to get in and pleading for supplies.

Inside, we learned it was a Jesuit monastery the aid workers were using for shelter and to stockpile supplies. Because of the limited amount of light, I could not see the details of the building. The brother in charge of the monastery greeted us and pointed out it was not safe to sleep inside the structure due to the many cracks on the walls, which were becoming more noticeable with the periodic aftershocks. They ordered us to sleep in small tents outside, away from the buildings.

The following morning, I awoke to a nightmare. There were domesticated animals freely roaming the premises—dogs, cats, hens, hogs, and goats. The monastery had a restricted supply of running water, and they closely rationed the time for us to freshen up. The brothers provided us with a basic breakfast buffet, military-style.

After a hasty briefing, the aid workers separated us into different groups by the corresponding specialty. I stayed with Scott and urged him to let me accompany him, at least for the first day. In the daylight, I could appreciate the physical condition of the massive monastery. There were cracks on all the walls, and the structure itself appeared to sway to one side. Every time I used the bathroom, I feared another earthquake collapsing the building while I was inside.

We drove through a sea of crumbled concrete. We could see what turned out to be piles of corpses covered in blankets in some corners as we passed by the dirty streets. Many public squares had become shantytowns. Lines of people waiting to get supplies stretched for miles. Meanwhile, bundles of food and water were sitting at the airport. It appeared people in Haiti would have to live a new existence, fighting every day to survive. There were hundreds of medical tents all over town.

The hospital they assigned us to was in total disarray. The French and the American medical teams were struggling, trying to figure out who was to remain in charge. After a few hours of tension, we moved to another medical facility not too far away. We reloaded our truck with all the supplies we had brought that morning. Once we settled in what appeared to have been an independent surgical center in an upscale section of town, we started our work. From a window on the second floor, I could see a U.S. Navy medical ship anchored a few miles from the harbor.

During the next ten days, I cared for many patients with crush injuries, most of which required amputations. Many of the patients had to withstand the painful operation with minimal anesthesia, consisting mainly of intravenous acetaminophen, the only sedative available. Amazingly, none of them screamed or complained while the manual saw cut through the bone. They accepted their condition and kept the dreadful pain to themselves. While the surgeon was performing the surgery, and I was assisting, I could not take my eyes off the patients' faces, frozen with acceptance and exhaustion from the horrendous pain. I never heard one of them moan.

During the duration of my stay in Haiti, I was overcome with emotions and a feeling of helplessness. After a while, I had to numb myself to everything. It was the only way to keep working. I felt distant and dissociated from the anguish. Time was distorted, and a profound emptiness overcame me. I had a hard time empathizing with the patients' feelings. Once I returned home, I had to dive into strenuous exercise and rigorous physical training to drown those feelings of temporary disconnection from my body and the outside world.

We left Haiti on a Wednesday morning after waiting for a U.S. military plane that could get us back to the United States. We were anxious because it could take several days before we would get on one of the military airplanes, which were flying missions back to the United States with hundreds of refugees seeking asylum. I was ready to leave the island as rapidly as possible. Feelings of regret and even anger inundated my mind. I felt like I couldn't cite anything of significance I had achieved after ten days in Port-au-Prince. The human tragedy I witnessed drove me to question my faith, and my religious convictions were growing blurry in my mind.

The military was not publicizing the ultimate destination of the flights taking off for the United States. At that moment, I didn't care. I just wanted to touch down in the United States, even if we landed in California. Once they called our names, we grabbed our packs and remained in line. During the next several hours, I reflected on my life and its significance. I made a promise to myself; once home, I would start a sincere exploration of my life's purpose. I also focused my efforts on a quest to encounter God outside my formal Catholic education.

Suffering of this magnitude has a poignant way of bringing your life and your convictions into perspective. I didn't know where to begin. How can a loving God allow such misery and injustice? These people had a hard life already, and this was hoisted on them undeservedly. This is also a profoundly religious country, with many people praying daily. I questioned if this pointed to a random existence dependent on the whims of chance. If true, that would remove all sense of significance or purpose. I felt despondent, confused, and irritated by these thoughts. All my efforts to improve my body and mind seemed pointless. Without a long-term perspective available, what was the point of overcoming anything? How was I to inspire or motivate? What could I tell my children about the future, their lives, or their motivation to go on?

In his work, "The Problem of Pain," C. S. Lewis confronts some of these questions. He makes a convincing argument that freedom of will cannot exist without the reality of suffering. The possibility for pain is the demonstration of infinite love by a Creator that wants to be loved without compulsion. And it is through pain that his creation can express that endless love to one another. God is all-capable of what is inherently possible, not of nonsense. There cannot be a free will without the possibility of wrong choices or in a world where all possibility of adversity is removed. These nuanced thoughts, however, were lost on me in the face of the horrors I had experienced and how it had shaken me to the core.

I found the inspiration I was seeking in an unanticipated place. Before my trip to Haiti, I had been looking for a challenging marathon somewhere exotic. For the last four years, I had been studying Machu Picchu, Peru, with an eye toward running the Inca Trail. I can't recall why, but I became obsessed with high altitude running, expecting it would bring me closer to God.

For ages, people have sought God in high places. The Old Testament is rich with stories of God's people, such as Abraham, Moses, and Elijah, finding and speaking to God on the top of mountains. I came as far as sending an application several times, but excuses and my debilitating fears discouraged me from finishing the process of signing-up for running the Inca Trail in Peru. Until finally one day, no more excuses.

CHAPTER 18

ULTRA!

BY THE FALL of 2011, I had signed up for an Inca Trail Marathon in Machu Picchu. I chose a tour company named Andes Adventures for the trip based on its reviews online.

The brochure announced the adventure of a lifetime. Devy, the owner of the travel company, specialized in running and hiking adventures in South America. It was an annual event. They described Peru as one of the most magnificent countries on the planet.

But the glossy advertising came with a warning. Participants needed to be physically and mentally in top shape for the trip. The announcement was for travelers with an adventurous spirit and a receptive mind. The terrain, the altitude, and the steep ascents and descents made the Machu Picchu a truly "ultra" marathon.

Then they cautioned about the risk of getting a condition called altitude sickness or in Quechua, *soroche*, which could spoil the trip. High altitude sickness is a medical condition produced by hypoxia, a reduction of oxygen while visiting places above 5,000 feet. The symptoms range from headaches, light-headedness, and dizziness to shortness of breath. I had experienced these before—every time I suffered a panic attack.

Running a marathon, merely my second one since I started running, high in the Peruvian Andes, was sounding like a not-so-splendid idea.

I imagined running an adventure marathon was like a metaphor for life: you need to prepare and know your purpose if you hope to succeed. That includes reading and studying, along with physical as well as mental preparedness. However, how you handle unforeseen situations comes from within.

I concluded the Inca Trail Marathon would be more than just a race. I wanted it to be a personal mission of self-discovery, personal growth, and hopefully achievement. I was determined to break away from the fears and doubts which had been holding me back throughout my life.

I understood that running a high-altitude marathon would require a substantial commitment. It would also take an extraordinary amount of mental courage and discipline. Regardless of how qualified I was physically, it would be one of the most challenging tests of my life.

The Inca Trail is a famous expedition with over 26 miles of subtropical jungles, mountains with altitudes ranging from 8,000 to 13,799 feet, as well as ancient ruins and tunnels built by the Incas in the 15th century. It calls for a considerable amount of preparedness and training.

The purpose of my training became an eagerness to get the most out of this unique experience by challenging my physical and mental fitness. I wanted to test my limits but also show the world my courage and resolve. No matter the great shape I was in, I had almost no outdoor experience. Trekking up the Andes would be nothing like running the 10K Turkey Trot or the Disney Marathon. Besides the complexity of their terrain, the Andes are mythical. They attract scores of New Agers seeking a more reliable connection to their spiritual beings. I even thought about hooking up with a Shaman and maybe booking a session while I was in Peru. I was hoping desperately for personal harmony and convergence in this place, on this trip.

For my physical training, I enlisted the services of one of my practice's senior physical therapists who had experience in the training of high-level athletes using high concentrations of oxygen.

After devoting some time with him, describing what I wanted to achieve, Dr. Jim (he was a doctor of allopathic medicine, chiropractic medicine, and physical therapy) and I developed a close relationship. Without additional compensation, he committed his time and effort to help me succeed.

As part of my preparation, he gave me a copy of a one-page paper he had written several years before on the subject of high concentration oxygen training. It was a case study entitled: Hyperoxia Training on a 37-Year-Old Male Duathlete. They published it in a medical periodical in 2005. He concluded that hyper-oxygen training could prepare me for a high-altitude race.

During the Vietnam War Jim served in the Navy as a medical corpsman, an experience that he credited with helping him discover his authentic vocation for healing the human body. This passion for healing guided Jim through the years to earn prestige and advanced qualifications in physical therapy and chiropractic medicine. His life's work ranged from sports medicine with professional athletes, to teaching and clinical investigation at the university level, to aid in the recovery of spinal surgery patients.

Jim worked on spinal surgery patients with a full day schedule for years despite having cancer, and he was always thankful to all who understood that his talents and his devotion to healing transcended his battle with cancer. He repeatedly told me he wanted to be remembered for his life's work and not for his death. He hoped that his family, friends, patients, students, and loved ones would celebrate his life in their own fashion, reflecting the impact that his military experience had on his life and the lives of those around him.

Besides his training in allopathic medicine, Jim also had a particular attraction to homeopathic medicine and we both shared a fascination for the spiritual power of healing. I will never forget our many conversations after work about the importance of the spirit in the practice of medicine. He always offered a piece of positive advice, and I was convinced he genuinely cared for me.

He took responsibility for the ultimate success of my running adventure. Within a few weeks of discussing my ambition to run a high-altitude marathon in Machu Picchu, Peru, he produced a personalized training program for me and volunteered to supervise my training personally. Jim did a preliminary test of my aerobic capacity and overall fitness before beginning my training regime.

His protocol comprised a five-minute warm-up on the treadmill, followed by 30 minutes of high-intensity interval training, and concluding with a five-minute cooldown. He provided oxygen through a non-rebreathing oxygen mask attached to an oxygen concentrator.

The 30-minute training intensity was set at 90 percent of my pre-test heart rate of 175 bpm. I was supposed to complete 18 training sessions, three sessions per week for six weeks. After my initial three weeks, as customary for me, I came up with excuses to lessen my training regimen. I missed the opportunity to have Jim with me during my training sessions.

The possibility that I might sustain a severe injury during the marathon troubled him, and he even mentioned the potential risk of dying. Jim called me often to know how I was making out. I suppose I didn't grasp the importance of training properly for this physical and mental challenge. Even worse, I missed the last opportunity of connecting with Jim before his untimely death.

I started conditioning my lower body by climbing stairs in a loop at home and at work. I tried to imagine being in Peru, traversing many miles over rugged terrain with slopes and challenging climbs. From my research, I knew the Incas constructed many trails with many miles of long and steep staircases, which posed a demanding physical challenge, especially at altitudes above 8,000 feet. I also used a weighted backpack to step up the intensity of my training pace. I thought I would have to carry my supplies, such as extra clothing, food, and water, which could add 30 pounds during my run.

In Florida, it was virtually impossible to find local trails with hilly terrain to hike. I had to focus my training on my aerobic conditioning to enhance my overall fitness. Running became my primary way of exercise to improve my agility, endurance, and strength. I continued with my strength training exercises at the gym to improve my upper and lower body conditioning. I put extra focus on strengthening my leg muscles with lunges, squats with weights, and deadlifts.

Running a high-altitude marathon is a significant commitment to make to yourself. I ran my first and only flat marathon a few years back with little training or preparation. I realized quickly that just a positive mental attitude is not enough. The mental fight doesn't begin until your body fails, mainly the last six miles, when every step turns into a little piece of hell, and every mile seems to last an eternity.

To prepare for the Inca Trail Marathon, I also started a program of mental conditioning. I had to imagine all the various scenarios that could go wrong and mentally prepare to address them. How does one train his mind for an event of more than 26 miles over three mountain passes at over 13,000 feet in the Andes Mountains of Peru?

During that time I got introduced by Tony Robbins to a book titled "Psycho-Cybernetics," written by a plastic surgeon and psychologist, Dr. Maxwell Maltz. His book was full of powerful ways to reach your full mental capacities and he introduced the seven elements of a personality concept that could attract success.

One of them caught my attention immediately, and I found it especially à propos to my pre-marathon training. It was courage. He defined courage as taking calculated risks to make your goals happen. He strongly advised to not delay taking action until you were confident. Even imperfect courage was better than none, he concluded. This book became my psychological guide to prepare for my audacious adventure.

I left the house on a Friday morning. The entire family gathered outside to say goodbye and wish me good luck. It was an emotional farewell for me, full of second thoughts and hesitation. My adventure started right away—at the airport. I had been reviewing the ten-page single-line pre-departure information document for the last few months. The checklist was impressive, going from required documents, check-in procedures, emergency contact phone numbers, luggage restrictions, money, tipping, travel insurance, weather, medical information, food and water, high altitude sickness, including Acute Mountain Sickness (AMS), electricity, email and phone communications, and all the accessories for the one night of camping before the marathon.

The flight from Miami to Peru was uneventful. I could see through the window while flying high over Peru, the clouds occasionally pierced by green mountain peaks. I stayed at an airport boutique hotel during my first night in the country. The following morning an Andes Adventures representative greeted me at the lobby of the hotel and took me and my heavy luggage to my connecting one-hour flight to Cusco.

Cusco was the ancient capital of the Inca Empire and the continent's oldest inhabited city.

When I arrived, two representatives were already waiting to take me to the hotel where the staff provided a traditional welcome cup of coca leaf to help with acclimatization to the 11,150 feet altitude.

I was excited to have my first taste of coca tea. It was supposed to give you energy, improve your stamina, and be a powerful antidote for altitude sickness. Although made from coca leaves, it's a long way off from the highly-priced end product, cocaine. Initially, I didn't notice any difference, but a few minutes later, I experienced a small buzz, a slight tingling on the tip of my tongue, followed by a sense of clear-headedness. At that moment, I regretted not having taken advantage of the opportunity for a session with a local Shaman and to experiment with Ayahuasca, a legal natural psychedelic drug derived from plants.

I met the rest of the group during a welcome lunch prepared by our primary guide, Devy. It was a brilliant mix of runners of different nationalities and exciting personalities. We were 33 runners, 19 from the U.S., three Australians, three New Zealanders, five Canadians, and one Spaniard.

Abelardo and Freddy were the two locals who were our assigned guides for the duration of the trip. They were both experienced runners and naturally accustomed to the high altitude.

After exchanging introductions and pleasantries for a few minutes, I discovered a minor detail I had missed when I signed up for the race. These people were experienced and high-level runners in search to complete an ultra marathon on a different continent. The prefix *ultra* was meaningless to me. I immediately connected with Apolo, the Spanish runner who took the time to explain what an ultra marathon meant.

When I learned an ultra-marathon meant a longer race than the regulatory length of 26.219 miles or 42.195 kilometers, my entire world came to a stop. They set the Inca Trail Ultra Marathon for 27.5 miles or 44.257 kilometers. Even though it didn't sound like an enormous difference, I immediately panicked and started drinking more of the coca tea. There wasn't much restful sleep that night.

After the welcome lunch, the group enjoyed a guided tour of the city. We visited the Cathedral, Qorikancha, the most important temple of the Inca Empire, and the Santo Domingo Monastery. We finished the day with a lovely dinner and overnight in Cusco.

The following morning we visited the archeological sites surrounding Cusco, beginning with the fortress and temple of Sacsayhuaman. The temple perched on a hillside overlooking Cusco at 12,136 feet. Even to this day, it's a mystery how the fortress was built. Huge stones, some of them weighing 125 tons, are carved into huge trapezoidal blocks that fit together with incredible precision.

Following the tour, we took off running downhill. It was our first 4.5-mile acclimatization run. On our way back to the city, we passed the village of Yuncaypat and the Temple of the Moon, finishing at the Plaza de Armas. My first run went exceptionally well. I finished among the first to cross our imaginary finish line with no hint of high-altitude sickness.

Cusco is a fascinating city, full of old charm and an amalgam of Native and European cultures. All the streets are inclined, so you are always ascending or descending. It reminded me of Seville with the narrow streets and the incessantly honking klaxons, a loud warning to stay on the sidewalks, away from the streets, and a reminder to watch your back. We found stray dogs and local vendors. The town buzzed with tourists from around the globe, wanderers recording everything with their fancy cameras. Machu Picchu is top of the bucket list for many seasoned travelers. At every intersection, it seemed, there was a Catholic church overlaid by Spaniards atop an Incan temple.

Cusco is located in a valley surrounded by steep hills on all sides. Just walking the streets was a great training exercise for the challenge I would face on the Inca Trail. I couldn't avoid noticing that none of the natives had a serious weight problem, as we have in the US. Their lean faces and bodies told the story of their hard work and long days. They all looked proud and happy.

The next morning we met a bus in front of our hotel lobby. We were headed on a scenic drive to Urubamba, the Sacred Valley of the Incas. We rode over a high plain with splendid views of the Cordillera Urubamba to the ancient Inca town of Chinchero, which sits at an elevation of 12,350 feet.

There we started our second acclimatization run, beginning on relatively flat terrain, passing through the salt mines of Maras, and finishing down at a scenic trail leading to the Urubamba River. The total distance was eight miles. By now I had already met all the rest of the runners. I became good friends with a couple from Australia, Pete and Donna.

I was so impressed with my ability to run at such a high altitude, I even filmed the run with my new GoPro camera and put together a music video with the help of my friend Pete. I published it on YouTube.

On day four we visited the villages of Ollanta and Ollantaytambo, the best surviving examples of an Inca town. Most of its buildings were built atop Inca walls, and the street plan is still the original created by the Inca builders. We could appreciate the Inca agricultural terraces creating small tiers of fertile land on very steep slopes. That day's run was optional, but although few people were interested, Apolo convinced me to run with him. He had missed the first few runs because of stomach problems.

Apolo was the athlete with the most experience, and they predicted him to win the marathon and possibly establish a record. He was the author of two books, one of them titled "Eight Skills to Deal with Eight Marathons." He had competed in sports challenges on five continents. He had swum across the Strait of Gibraltar, completed Ironman triathlons, the Trans-Tibetan Mountain Bike, and multiple marathons in different environments, including Kilimanjaro and now Machu Picchu. Even with these impressive credentials, he felt that I was the person to beat.

Besides Apolo, there were other experienced runners with extensive accomplishments in the group. Most of them were completing their sixth ultra-marathon on their sixth continent. We had Amanda, a geologist from New Zealand, who was an accomplished book author and well-known and experienced marathoner. She had just completed the Great Wall of China Marathon in four hours. After Machu Picchu, she was scheduled for an extreme marathon in the jungles of the Amazon. The more I interacted with other runners, the more I realized my misplacement and lack of preparation.

The following day we traveled by bus to the trailhead at 82 Piscacucho, where we began our run to km 88 Qoriwayrachina. After entering the Machu Picchu Sanctuary National Park, we were just a mile away from our camp in the archeological site of Llactapata, a "Town on Hillside" at 8,400 feet. I was expecting a peaceful evening enjoying hot coca tea and a splendid view of the Urubamba mountain range. Our last assignment before the great day was a low pace six and a half-mile run along the Urubamba River. I used this opportunity to reflect on my trip so far—what I had learned about myself and what I had learned from all the incredible people I was meeting. On that run, I felt close to my Creator.

Up to this point, I had been spared the stomach aches many of my compatriots had suffered, including my roommate—a young and fit man almost 20 years my junior. He had traveled the entire world pursuing his passion for running different terrains and environments in different countries.

After a delicious and colorful dinner that night, we all retired to our tents to rest to prepare for the main event the following morning. We were supposed to all meet at the starting line no later than 5:30 a.m.

Around 2:30 a.m. I woke with a terrible stomachache and nausea. I had to go outside to vomit. The place where we were camping had no outside restrooms. I had to arm myself with courage and go to the base of the mountain in the middle of the darkness with howling wolves to vomit and squat in a desolated area with violent diarrhea.

I didn't want to wake up anyone, knowing we have to be at the starting line by 5:30 a.m. after breakfast. I was scared and fearful about not being able to start the marathon after everything I had done to get here. I felt weak and shaky. My anxiety and fears mounted. After 30 minutes outdoors I returned to my tent and could only sleep a few hours before the alarm went off and a few of our guides began their routine of waking each one of us and announcing breakfast was ready.

Since waking at 4 a.m. I had braved 45-degree temperatures, stomach pain, nausea, profuse sweating, a sore throat from vomiting, a blinding headache, and a feeling I had bit off more than I could chew. Suddenly I was overpowered by a sense of impending doom and failure.

I said to myself, "How can I quit now?" I knew I was the least trained and one of the oldest in the group, but this was going to be my first ultra!

CHAPTER 19

THE INCA TRAIL

AFTER A RESTLESS two hours of sleep in my tent, I woke up at 4 a.m. to a spectacular sky sprinkled with stars. It was chilling. Everybody gradually got ready and headed for the breakfast tent before proceeding to the start line. I showed up at the tent when breakfast was already served, but I chose only to try the coffee.

I consumed my fair amount of bottled water, perceiving I was probably dehydrated from my previous night of frequent puking and diarrhea. I was still nauseous, weak, and dizzy. I told Abelardo, our knowledgeable local guide who has run the Inca Trail over 100 times, what I had gone through overnight. He urged me to drink plenty of coca tea instead of coffee and to chew several leaves for a few minutes, keeping a few to chew for later. For it to be effective, he said, the leaves had to dissolve thoroughly in my mouth.

Devy met with the group for an essential pre-marathon briefing. He furnished us maps of the route and pointed out the location of the aid stations scattered along the trail.

Then in a solemn tone, he said, "In the history of this marathon we have had no one with a broken bone." He went on, "However, we lost a runner for three days after he made the wrong turn on one path." He added, "Most of the time, the trail is easy to follow, but there are two or three places where people could go off course."

He reminded us about the lack of medical aid or rescue personnel and the waiver we had just signed. We needed to pay attention to our surroundings and to follow the signs carefully. Devy was planning on remaining with the leaders, and Abelardo would continue in the middle with the mid-pack racers.

Finally, a third person, Eddie, a licensed guide and experienced high-altitude trail runner, would continue with the last one of the group until the finish line. Devy emphasized the entrance to Machu Picchu would close by 4 p.m. and any of us who could not make it by that time would have to walk the railroad tracks to Aguas Calientes to meet them at the hotel which would add another two hours to the time of arrival.

Also, you wouldn't be able to claim you had completed the marathon. He acted as though this was extremely improbable because we were leaving at 5:30 in the morning. After hearing this, and doing some mental calculations, my heart began racing and my anxiety and fears crept up. I realized I had to finish the marathon in ten hours or less.

My chest felt tight, and my lungs felt almost like I was taking on water—like I was drowning. I calmed myself down by listening to the music selection I had previously chosen for this moment that was playing on my iPhone. I glanced around to see if I would be the last one to finish. I said to myself if I was, Eddie would have to stick around with me for the entire duration of the run, reducing the chances of me getting lost. I didn't have a GPS with me as the others did.

I remembered there was a gentleman called John, five years older than me, who perhaps would be the last one. I arrogantly sized him up, thinking he looked frail. My ego wouldn't let him beat me.

All of us, a diverse group of individuals, most of whom were experienced ultra-marathon runners from all parts of the world, aligned at the start. I recall two particular runners next to me.

Mitchell, a 30-year-old stockbroker from Atlanta, had already completed 15 marathons in the last six months and was in top physical shape for this one. Doris, from Nevada, had been a professional runner for most of her life. Now, in her early 60s, she had retired to become a sports columnist for a running magazine. She would write a column about this race and our adventure. Recently, she had completed the 100-mile Death Valley Ultra.

It was still pitch dark when we started the marathon. Fortunately, I had packed for survival: headlamp, hand flashlight, two energy bars, a few power gels, a brand new 70-ounce Camelbak hydration system, a hat, sunglasses, and my GoPro camera with its head attachment in place. I started running at a good pace to stay with the pack.

I depended on my fellow runners to light the trail with their mighty handheld flashlights and headlights. I was astonished to bump, so early in the day, into porters and mules descending the road. I have to admit, after six days of high altitude living, I was frazzled. But I was also excited and thrilled about this rare opportunity, even in the darkness.

I thought about how I would certainly be motivated by the beauty and mysticism of the scenes unfolding before me slowly under the rising sun.

The first three miles took us along the Cusichaca River, leaving behind the Urubamba valley. In front of us was an impressive view of snow-capped Mount Veronica (18,865 feet), the highest peak in the Urubamba mountain range. Suddenly, a few feet in front of me, I spotted Mitchell being aided by Devy and several porters. He looked pale and in obvious respiratory distress.

Later on, I found out he had to leave the marathon because of a severe case of high altitude sickness. My mind wondered about how this fit and much younger guy was suddenly so sick. He had been preparing for this trip for so long and training so hard it was impossible to comprehend. I feared what was next.

Despite this, and after making sure that he was medically stable, I went on running, hoping I could remain in the race.

As I climbed further up the mountain, the sun rose high enough that it began to illuminate the surrounding valley. The roosters signaled the beginning of a new day, and the smell of freshly brewed coffee coming from different campsites was like a magnet drawing me in its direction. By this time I was not running, but power walking. My legs already felt heavy, tired, and sluggish.

After a while, we arrived at the village of Wayllabamba at 9,100 feet, the last inhabited village on the Inca trail. In my mind, I had reached the point of no return. By that time, I was making numerous halts to recover my breath. However, I was still not the last runner.

As I continued to climb, the trail turned into a more difficult challenge. I penetrated the spectacular LLulluchayoc Gorge and the path became steeper as I entered mossy woods. The climb continued uphill through a thick jungle before emerging into a broad meadow LLulluchapampa at about 12,400 feet.

I caught a second wind and conjured the Inca Gods. I reached the Waemiwasnusq'a pass, "Pass of the Dead Woman," at 13,799 feet, the highest pass in the Inca Trail. I barely made it to the top when I saw John pass me by. I was the last runner. Next to me, Eddie grinned sarcastically. "I think you're the last one now," he said.

I gathered myself, sipped some water, and got a bite of one of my protein bars. I began the short rocky descent into the valley which took me up to the Pacaymayo River. I started to wonder who would recover my body and ship it back to my family in the U.S. from here. Mercifully, I spotted our first aid station. It was an excellent excuse to sit and rest for 20 minutes without annoying Eddie. He already doubted I would finish the marathon within the allotted window, and he reminded me several times about the need to reach Machu Picchu's entrance before 4 p.m.

While I was resting, Eddie received a message on his radio reporting a grave injury to one of our leading runners. It was Doris, who had taken a nasty fall around mile 12, hitting her head against some rocks and also breaking her right hand, struggling to stop her free fall down a precipice with no guardrails. Two porters had to carry her on a rudimentary stretcher back 14 miles by foot to a local clinic in Aguas Calientes. The clinic only had basic radiographs and no orthopedic surgeon on staff. I instantly worried about her and the prospect of a subdural hematoma, which, if left untreated, could kill her. The closest CT Scan was in Lima, a two-hour plane ride. But, as Devy warned us in the beginning, the marathon had to continue, and no medical helicopter appeared to rescue her.

I steeled myself for what was left, ascending a steep set of big and wide steps toward Runkurakay Pass. On the way there, I came across the Runkurakay watchtower ruins at 12,464 feet—another excuse for me to slow down and catch my breath. Finally, I arrived at the Runkurakay Pass at 13,000 feet. I was content to hear Eddie say most of the climb was behind us.

I enjoyed the magnificent views of the glaciated peaks of the Cordillera Vilcabamba. From there on, the trail descended rocky slopes, ultimately reaching the vital fortress of Sayacmarca, "The Dominant Town," at 12,234 feet. Beyond this point, an impressive Inca road appeared in front of me.

The six-foot-wide and laboriously constructed stone-paved trails are a testament to the fantastic Inca road construction. An incredible engineering achievement.

Suddenly I was in front of a 20-meter Inca tunnel with carved granite steps turning into a magnificent stone staircase leading to Puyupatamarca, "Town in the Clouds," at 11,674 feet. I barely made it to our third pass and had my first look into the deep gorge of the Urubamba River. The last aid station was just below, by the ruins of Puyupatamarca. The trail went down a series of hundreds of steps, passing by ceremonial Inca baths, where still mountain water flows down through ingeniously carved stone channels.

As I continued to descend the uneven and never-ending steps, I became surrounded by a wide variety of exotic plants and animals until I eventually reached the ruins of Winya Wayna, "Forever Young." It was at this moment when Eddie realized the entrance to Machu Picchu would probably be closed for the day when we finally arrived. Once again, Eddie was correct. When we reached the rear entrance, the sign on the fence read that the park was closed. Please come back tomorrow. However, an agent at the admission control entrance was still on duty.

Eddie calmly asked me to wait, and he proceeded ahead to persuade him to allow us to continue through. After at least ten minutes of intensive negotiations, Eddie came back to inform me of the outcome. He said I was good to go through the gate, but unless I was injured the guides had to stay behind.

Eddie is not easily deterred. He strategized with me.

"You pretend you've got back pain," he said. "But sell it. Like it's awful."

There was a youthful, muscular porter nearby whom Eddie convinced to carry me over the threshold. As long as it seemed like I required the help I could go through the gate.

I knew this meant I would be disqualified. I was disappointed and humiliated, and it almost made the hours of struggle seem fruitless. But, as I said, Eddie doesn't give up easily.

"If you don't mention this to anyone, my lips are sealed forever," he offered. "Let's just make sure we leave a hefty tip for the guy."

I happily agreed and I did as Eddie said. It was the best performance of my non-existent acting career. I writhed in pain. It wasn't hard for me to do. My bones ached and my back had spasmed from time to time. The porter lifted me by my legs and threw me over his shoulder. The rest was short-lived, though.

Once we made a turn and the officer couldn't see us any longer, the youthful and muscular guy dropped me like a sack of potatoes. From there, we still had about three and a half miles to Intipunku, the famous "Gateway of the Sun" at 8,860 feet. The arduous climb up the practically vertical steps took about 80 minutes. I had to crawl on all fours, clinging onto the steps for my life.

Once I arrived at the Sun Gate, suddenly the full grandeur of the world's greatest Inca ruins was revealed. As Mark Adams described in his novel "Turn Right at Machu Picchu," the ancient city was "laid out before the visitor like a Lego metropolis atop a billiard table." It took me a few minutes to realize I was in the presence of one of the world's most incredible archeological discoveries.

I knew I was close to the finish line. I was wondering if anybody would be there to greet me and accompany me back to the hotel. With the end in sight, an adrenaline rush catapulted me the last kilometer until I cleared the final steps and was greeted by my Australian friend, Pete, who had finished his marathon in nine hours, and stuck around for me while the rest of the runners headed back to the hotel. My time: 11 hours and four minutes.

There is something incredibly thrilling about doing something you never thought you could. Whether it's an athletic goal, an academic goal, a career goal, or a creative goal, there's no better way to expand your belief in yourself than to undertake an ambitious goal and achieve it. For people like marathon runners, there is a particular thrill in the fact that the process can be difficult and painful. In some ways, running a marathon is an excellent training and testing ground for other life skills. It's challenging and it's painful, but you *know* that your body will adapt as you push yourself and the moment you cross the finish line is a concrete moment of achievement.

In this way, running a marathon is like achieving any goal. But unlike reaching your career or creative goals, you know it's possible. You know what to expect, and you know exactly when it's finished.

A growing body of research shows that there's wisdom in the marathon runner's embrace of difficulty and discomfort. The idea that "what doesn't kill you makes you stronger" really seems to be true—but the way we approach difficulty and discomfort also matters. You may have encountered two common ways of looking at difficulty, challenges, and discomfort in the world. Some people seem to think these things are *always* wrong, leading to adverse outcomes. Others behave as though they are always *good,* leading to greater strength. It turns out that, just like with diet, "all things in moderation" is a good motto when it comes to hardship and adversity. People who report having experienced *some* hardship turn out to have higher resilience to adversity and higher overall happiness than *either* those who have never experienced hardship or those who have experienced extreme trauma.

This may be linked to the ability of difficulty and discomfort to act as learning grounds for coping mechanisms. People who endure *some* difficulty and discomfort, without becoming uncontrollably overwhelmed, may learn psychological and neurological regulatory mechanisms that allow them to modulate their moods and their experience of distress better in the future.[26]

The technique of exposure therapy may hold other secrets to achievement through adversity. By helping people to experience their phobias and traumas in a gradual, safe, controlled manner, this type of therapy can train the nervous system to handle this stress and create significant improvements in the well-being of people with PTSD.[27]

People who experience adversity in a controlled way may also learn the most crucial lesson of hardship—that you can view it as a threat or an opportunity.

People who see obstacles as threats, or as indicators of things they "can't" do, are less likely to achieve high performance or high life satisfaction. On the other hand, people who view obstacles and hardships as opportunities to grow or puzzles to be solved are less likely to be overwhelmed with painful emotions, and more likely to find ways to come out on top in challenging times.[28]

The wisdom of the marathon runners is this—they know that undertaking challenging goals that require pushing through discomfort is a way to personal growth. By embracing hardship in a controlled and (relatively) safe manner, they expand their abilities to cope with discomfort and doubt, and they come out happy and victorious on the other side.

---

26 Seery, M. D., Holman, E. A., & Silver, R. C. (2010). Whatever does not kill us: Cumulative lifetime adversity, vulnerability, and resilience. *Journal of Personality and Social Psychology, 99*(6), 1025-1041. doi:10.1037/a0021344

27 Coping with Adversity: New psychological research from Teachers College. (2016, November 15). Retrieved May 19, 2020, from https://www.tc.columbia.edu/articles/2016/november/psychology-of-adversity/

28 Hall, K. (2016, May 12). Overcoming Obstacles. Retrieved May 19, 2020, from https://www.psychologytoday.com/us/blog/pieces-mind/201605/overcoming-obstacles

CHAPTER 20

THE FINISH LINE

THE SUN SCORCHED my bare face, and I could barely lift my feet to climb the last step. I thought I might have died. As if from a dream, I awoke on top of an imposing city submerged in clouds, and I said to myself, if I have died, I've gone to heaven.

The entire world paused for a few moments. I soaked in one of the planet's most impressive sites. My miseries dissolved like the clouds through my fingers.

My previous fears and anxieties now belonged to a past I never wanted to repeat. I embraced this opportunity to pray and praise God for allowing me to arrive at the promised land. My pride and my need to be recognized was no longer my driving force. I had never been timid about singing my praises, but now I was uncharacteristically silent about this personal triumph. I felt embraced by a doting power vaster than me. I could feel my expression change from the outward mask I have always worked to deal with life into an expression of my true being.

Many times the desire to be recognized gives birth to alienation and unhappiness. The ego swallows the rest of the self. We are obstructed by the power to prove self-sufficiency to others instead of enjoying our gifts for ourselves.

Atop Machu Picchu, I could see everything. I was able to observe my insatiable anxiety and my hedonistic desire to cover up my shortcomings. Breathing in the clouds, I could appreciate how wearing and distressing my attitudes had become. I stretched my arms out to the sky as if the chains were falling open off my wrists. I could be my genuine self atop the mountain, free of this world's trappings.

Survival wasn't the ultimate goal anymore. It became transcendence. I decided at that moment to own my destiny. I said to myself, I said to myself, "imagine what you can accomplish if you just refuse to fail." I promised from now on not to let my fears and attachment to outcomes guide my decisions.

Of all the things that could have appeared in my mind's eye just then, what I saw was my father. I had departed Florida without telling him about the adventure I was about to undertake. I thought if I told him, he would have scolded me and guilted me into canceling the trip. He was in his late 80s and frail by then. He was somewhat independent, but he lived in a retirement home, fragile and needy. It occurred to me that he could pass away while I was scaling Machu Picchu and that I would never tell him this story. The thought dampened my celebration.

The truth is, though, that a fear or guilt-driven action like canceling my trip based on my father's caprices would have crippled my capacity to evolve. My father had enjoyed a carefree, sometimes reckless existence in pursuing new experiences to enjoy and appreciate, even at the expense of his family. We had our disagreements and conflicts, and we approached the world differently. He could be selfish and even aloof. He was not as ambitious as I was, and he took his health for granted, while I struggled to take care of mine.

As he aged, he never forgave me for having taken his car away. He was in his early 80s when my brother and I decided it was time for him to move into an assisted living facility without the car. Regardless of how luxurious the place we found for him was, he always called it his gilded cage.

On top of the mountain, the resentment and anger I harbored in my heart for all those years vanished in the wind. Instead, I focused on his infectious smile, his witty and often irreverent sense of humor, and especially his resolve, when he chose at a young age to live his life on his terms. I came to accept the fact that many of the things I enjoy so much in my life now are because of his influence. I couldn't hate him. I was liberated and ready to start a life of forgiveness.

The voice of my friend Pete congratulating me snapped me out of my trance. Emotions and feelings I could not describe at that moment overwhelmed me. After 11 hours of running and power walking a tough and long trail, I was physically exhausted and mentally drained. However, I still wanted to enjoy the beauty of Machu Picchu, particularly at this time of the day when the park was already closed and I could explore the astonishing landscape by myself. Running the Inca trail in one day is a huge accomplishment. Most hikers take an average of three days to complete it.

After a well-deserved rest I spent the entire next day with our experienced guides and the group, touring the mystical city of Machu Picchu, exploring its splendid temples, terraced hillsides, archeological curiosities, irrigation channels, fountains, elaborate stonework and many chambers of unknown purpose.

As I was listening to the stories about the mysteries of Machu Picchu, I wondered how and why this city was built in such a remote and difficult place. It thrilled me that my Spanish ancestors never discovered this magnificent citadel and that they never had the opportunity to destroy it.

That afternoon we headed back to our hotel, the Inkaterra Machu Picchu Pueblo Hotel, an intimate Andean village with terraced hills, waterfalls, stone pathways, and whitewashed adobe casitas tucked away in the cloud forest.

The property had 12 acres of exquisite natural beauty, where 214 bird species, such as the golden-headed quetzal and the iconic Andean cock-of-the-rock, and the world's most extensive native orchid collection (372 species) have been registered. It was the perfect hotel for relaxing.

The main entrance to the hotel inspires a sense of energy and a feeling of internal well-being regardless of what is happening around you. The property is surrounded by the dry branches of tall eucalyptuses. I immediately thought about my Forever Young, MD business and this hotel as the perfect backdrop for an anti-aging clinic.

The natural beauty of the Andean cloud forest is overwhelming. The hotel was landscaped naturally with vibrant orchids, exotic bromeliads, colorful butterflies, and hundreds of bird species, including many endemics I didn't have time or energy to appreciate while trying to survive the Inca Trail Marathon. That evening I took advantage of some free time before dinner to explore the hotel's beautiful nature. I reflected, opening my heart and my mind to the landscape, listening for God.

Near the head of the trail, I stopped to contemplate a majestic tree. I was listening to God in the branches, but I heard my mom: "Kiko, don't take risks. You know you are fragile and you don't have what it takes to handle the consequences of your careless actions." The heavy tree laughed off my mother's advice like a gentle breeze tickling its leaves. The past six days had been amazing. In the past, I had stopped myself from taking risks, inadvertently erecting obstacles to my happiness and fulfillment.

I wished I could take my mother on a walk through this nature trail. I wished I could go over the photographs from the top of Machu Picchu with her like an album of my accomplishments. Finally, I could show my worth—prove to her I was a capable person. Making her proud of me.

After an hour of deep reflection amid the splendid gardens, I headed back to the restaurant for our award ceremony dinner. I was eager to hear from Doris and find out if she was planning on returning to Lima. I was proud of our group of runners.

Throughout the trip, we encouraged each other when the going got tough. We developed a bond of friendship and teamwork that stayed with us throughout the journey. I have never met such an exciting group of intelligent and athletic people. There were no complainers, whiners, or slackers. The differences in age and nationality made it even more fascinating.

The restaurant was remarkable. The tables stood under a traditional Amazonian Ese'Eja palm-thatched roof, tastefully adorned with regional crafts. The food was a blend of Andean cuisine and Spanish tradition, fusion-style fare. It was the ultimate Peruvian cuisine with an elegant contemporary twist. The food pairing with local wines was exceptional and a delightful surprise. Besides the mesmerizing atmosphere, this first-class restaurant featured stunning views of the Vilcanota River.

Spending some time chatting with Doris reassured me she was doing fine both mentally and physically. She's an experienced writer, and she described her struggle eloquently. Amazingly, only a day later she recognized how lucky she was to be alive and surrounded by an incredible group of people who showed so much love and support to her.

She said to me, "Francisco, one thing I can take home from this experience is we need to appreciate life every day and focus on our relationships with others. We need to allow God and the universe to guide us always." She told me, "our fears and anxieties can be conquered if we believe in ourselves and recognize the purpose in everything that happens to us."

We wrapped up the night with the medal presentation. It was no surprise to us when Devy announced who had won the Ultra Marathon. It was Apolo, who completed the marathon in seven hours. The slide presentation playing in the background showed a proud Apolo, rolled up in a colorful Spanish flag, kissing the ground.

I believe in his mind he felt like he was doing what his ancestors failed to do, discover and conquer the lost Inca Palace. In my mind was the image of Francisco Pizarro, the Spanish conquistador who led to the fall of the Inca Empire and the Spanish conquest of Peru.

Atahualpa, the Inca Emperor, naively believed Pizarro and his men were demigods. What followed was the utter destruction of a magnificent civilization.

Mine was the last name called. The old me would have been embarrassed, but I was so proud to have endured, to be a part of something like this. I grinned at Eddie, acknowledging our pact of silence and loyalty to each other. Instead of giving him money, like I always did when trying to recognize outstanding service, I gave something more precious to him, my brand-new Camelbak Rogue Hydration Pack he had complimented during our time together. He had given me so much more.

CHAPTER 21

THE TRAIN RIDE HOME

TWO DAYS AFTER the marathon, we rose early for a three and a half-hour train ride back to Cusco. The journey recalled my first childhood experiences with trains. My companion on those first train rides in Spain had always been my brother. I remember one particular train ride I took with my brother when I was eight. Since it was a short ride, we traveled by ourselves from Seville to my mother's hometown, the small village of Rio Minas. I remember that trip as one of the best times of my life. Nestled beside my brother, I felt safe and loved. The rhythmic bouncing of the train was like being rocked to sleep in my mother's arms. We were not aware of the fact—nor would we have cared—that we rode third class. Sitting next to us were local villagers, some of them carrying live chickens and ducks. Despite the multitudes around us and the chaos, I strangely felt entirely at peace. Thinking back on that experience, I realize that it was an imprint that anchored in me a world view.

There are some memories from childhood that don't fade with time. They stick like a colored photograph clipped to the refrigerator—vivid and real. Later in life, like Proust's madeleine, the most prosaic sight or smell or sound can launch us right into our mind's photograph of the moment. Who says time travel isn't possible?

On that train ride in Peru, the trigger wasn't the soaring mountainscape or even the gentle rumbling of the train. It was the smell of salted sandwich meats. As a boy, the highlight of our train travels was the giddy unwrapping of the sandwiches my grandmother would prepare for us. Usually we got a Spanish omelet between the bread, but when we were lucky, my grandmother added strips of warm Jamón Serrano and chorizo. The scent was intoxicating on those journeys, filling my lungs with satisfaction.

Savoring these sandwiches, I would stare out the window and observe the landscape unfolding like a movie. With my eyes transfixed on the countryside, I could still listen with idle ears to the passengers' life stories. Though I didn't recognize at the time, this was truly a meditative state, a time where I was beginning to discover who I was.

As we passed the local rail stations, we could see travelers waiting on the quays, getting ready for their trips. We ripped through picturesque towns painted white and busy with residents going about their daily routines. I saw children dressed in uniforms going to school. Spain was all around me, but so was life. I was absorbing my environment in a new way. There was a certain majesty to the quotidian on these trips. The earth doesn't flower in Andalucía the way it does in the mountains of Peru, but the people sure do. The rhythmic swaying to the clickety-clack sound of the train entranced me, shaking my imagination free. It was not about how fast we could get to our ultimate destination. The train ride was a destination unto itself. The train in Peru rattled me out of my mind's eye when we came upon a heavy rainstorm.

The rain was surprising, just outside Aguas Calientes. El Niño had shown up for an unannounced visit, even though June is supposed to be Peru's dry season with virtually no rain in the forecast. But the forecast didn't mean much to El Niño, who had other plans for us. It had already started drizzling at the station as we boarded the train. The train picked up speed along the track, and the wind and the cold air quickened as well. The rain turned into sleet as we approached the first stone tunnel. Train rides in my memory were tranquil excitements of youth, but at that moment, I felt a very adult fear and worry about the dangers ahead. I imagined falling rocks or mudslides crushing the rickety train. As the train climbed up the mountainside, the sleet turned into hail.

I could feel my heart racing, and by now, I knew what I needed to do to avoid a full-blown panic attack. I searched the train car for something else on which to focus. A few rows in front of me, I noticed a young girl wearing a pair of silver earrings. The earrings were long and round with a shiny texture. They were just like the pair I had gifted Evelyn, a fifth-grade classmate back in Puerto Rico. The surrounding tempest faded into the background.

The year was 1973, and I was resolved to ask a girl to be my Valentine. I could feel my hormones starting to kick in, running through my emotions, and controlling my movements. In the past, just the thought of February would have led to a sense of alarm and anxiety too powerful for me to confront. The dreaded holiday terrified me because of the genuine prospect that I would be the only boy left in my grade without a Valentine. By fifth grade, I wanted to show the entire class that I, too, could enjoy this colorful celebration. Of course, I always imagined the other boys with some unique ability when dealing with girls—a skill I didn't have.

When I was in kindergarten, more than anything Valentine's Day was a popularity contest, where the students were thrilled to pass out handcrafted Valentine's cards, hoping to get an equal number in exchange. Some kids had put in long hours writing special notes to accompany a bag of Hershey's chocolate kisses. If you got fewer cards than "Juanito," you took it personally. The average kindergarten teacher tensed up and to ward off a disaster she always asked us to bring enough cards and bags of Hershey chocolate kisses for the entire class. Her exhortations didn't always work.

Middle school changed the entire playing field. Valentine's Day represented total anarchy at school. There were no more attempts from the teachers to even things out around the celebration—a lesson in survival of the fittest and natural selection. More than a popularity contest, it became an affirmation of not being loved or wanted if you didn't have a Valentine. In my mind, the reason for this was most likely because of your physical appearance or lack of external accomplishment. At this age, it is easy to feel everyone else is more loved than you are. This sentiment has the potential, as it did in my situation, to be carried on well into adulthood with dreadful repercussions.

For a long time, I had been secretly admiring a girl in my class named Evelyn. It was an intense platonic type of love, one-sided. Up to that moment, I had been reluctant and timid in approaching her. However, I had decided that this year would be different and I had to build up the courage to conquer my timidity. For this, I recruited my mom to take me to a local jewelry store and find a present for Evelyn. While in the store, my mother suggested a cheap pair of silver-plated earrings. I listened to her advice—what did I know about jewelry, after all? She told the salesperson it was a special present and asked him to wrap it with the obligatory heart-covered Valentine paper. I was enthusiastic but uneasy about going to school the following day to confront my dread of speaking to Evelyn.

After a restless night, I woke up with my heart in my throat. I felt my chest tighten, and I am not exaggerating when I say I had some trouble breathing. Again, a sense of drowning overwhelmed me. After I got dressed, deliberately selecting my uniform to be sure there were no blemishes or wrinkles, I snatched my backpack, my lunch box, and the earrings. That day my father uncharacteristically decided he wanted to drive us to school. Before dropping us off, he asked what I was carrying with me in the gift box. I reluctantly told him it was a Valentine's present for the teacher and ran out. I knew my dad was liable to make one of his sarcastic comments, which would have ruined the moment for me.

As the school bell rang, I ran to my homeroom to drop off the gift under my desk. I didn't want anyone to see me hiding the gift box with the earrings. The morning went relatively smoothly. Everybody looked sharp, and there was a general sense of celebration and joy in the air. I was desperately trying to figure out when would be the right moment to give Evelyn my gift. In the morning rush, I forgot to bring the Valentine card I had bought for her the previous day. But I went forward anyway, taking advantage of the morning recess. I approached Evelyn while she was still seated at her desk, picking up her books. Exchanging no words, I smiled nervously and placed the box with the earrings on her desk. She was speechless. I left her side and dashed to the back of the room.

The day went on as usual and when the dismissal bell rang, while walking toward the front door, I saw something unreal—Evelyn had already donned her earrings and looked at me with a big smile on her face. She looked so beautiful and content. I got so excited that instead of walking towards her, I ran outside to meet my mom. When she saw me, she asked with a grin on her face how it went. I just said it went well and I kept my mouth shut for the rest of the evening. I was enjoying a sense of accomplishment and I was dying to see Evelyn the next morning. I might even muster the courage to ask her about the earrings and how much she liked them. I truly believed it would be the beginning of a new stage in my life.

The next day I was impatient to go to school. I saw myself meeting Evelyn in front of the classroom, behaving like boyfriend and girlfriend, enjoying an intimate conversation. I told my mom I didn't want to waste time having breakfast and asked her vehemently to take me to school as soon as possible. With some reluctance, she agreed to leave for school at that unusually early hour.

When I arrived at school, I looked for Evelyn everywhere. After waiting patiently, the school bell summoned us all inside. I looked with sadness at Evelyn's seat, which was still empty. The entire day I could not think of anything else but Evelyn, wondering where she was. Did she skip school to avoid seeing me? It was a long and unproductive day.

I replaced all the excitement of the previous day with a sense of sadness and loss. When the time came to go home, I walked somberly towards the school entrance to meet my mother. Immediately I told her what happened, hoping for my mom's advice and support. She reassured me it was just a coincidence. She even suggested Evelyn might have gotten sick from eating too many Valentine's Day chocolates. As always, my mom's words gave me a sense of inner peace and hope.

The next day came, and still there was no sign of Evelyn.

In the afternoon, one of Evelyn's girlfriends walked over to me. She told me Evelyn had an allergic reaction to the earrings, and she had to be taken to the hospital. Evelyn was taking antibiotics and was ordered to rest for a few days. They expected her back to school in a few days. I was crestfallen. I felt immediately responsible for what happened to Evelyn. I couldn't help but remember Manolito from Spain—my best friend who got the mumps from me and died. I was cursed, condemned to hurt everyone I loved.

The day Evelyn returned to school she showed me the scar the earrings had made on her earlobe, and from then on I avoided her as much as I could.

As the train rattled on in Peru, barreling past a barrage of hail and wind, I smiled at that little boy in Puerto Rico, terrified that he could only hurt the things he loved. He was so easily saddened. He felt so alone, despite an army of people in his corner. There was absolute helplessness plastered on his face, and his heart was heavy—always so heavy. He was blind to everything he might accomplish. Everything he has accomplished.

It took a long time for that little boy in Puerto Rico to grow up. On my latest train ride, I felt he finally had.

Part of my happiness came from the sense of satisfaction I enjoyed from having conquered the ancient marathon in the mountains. But it wasn't everything. It wasn't even the principal thing.

In remembering how fragile I had been, I felt proud of how fragile I still am. That fragility isn't a flaw like I had been trained to think for so long. It's the thing that makes me special—the detail that colors all of my accomplishments in brightness. I haven't overcome my anxieties, but I've learned to harness them. It wasn't easy. But it can be done. I am a testament to that.

On the train racing through that storm, I was not afraid. I was grateful for my family, my children, and my wife, who stuck with me when I wasn't at my most adhesive. I was thankful for the other characters in my life who motivated me to keep kicking. I said a little prayer for Mr. Winston and his blonde assistant, Ms. Giovanini, that they might know what an impact they had on my life. I thought about my grandparents and my aunts in Spain, laboring clumsily but earnestly for my well-being. I dreamt of my parents, at peace with their fears, as they rest in a better place. I wanted nothing more than to finally rush home and live my new life with everyone I love.

"I have been bent and broken, but I hope, into a better shape."

—**Charles Dickens,
Great Expectations**

Prayer for Calmness

In the tempests of anxiety, adversity and desperation,
Be our stake in the ground, our unshakeable north star,
our shelter from elements, the loving Father of the World.
May we find courage in the seagulls, who glide on raging
winds, and the oceans, rolling back and forth in the storm.
May we follow the example of the redwood trees,
networking and nourishing each other invisibly beneath the
surface, so that groves may grow tall and scarlet and boundless.
Make us faithful brothers and sisters in the Family of all mankind,
So that in the morning we may celebrate together in Thanksgiving

F.M. Torres, M.D.

EPILOGUE
ANXIETY IN THE TIME OF CORONAVIRUS

I PLANNED TO end this book on the image of my fists raised triumphantly above my head, looking out at Machu Picchu from among the clouds. The symbolic summit of the mountain was going to be a neat punctuation mark for a journey that started with a boy afraid of drowning in the local pool. Fear and anxiety didn't stop me, and it doesn't have to stop you. The story had a nice arc.

If you struggle with anxiety, you know that as old fears die, new fears resurface, and even some old ones come back from the dead. There is no neat ending to a story about living with anxiety—only reliable tools and little victories.

Anxiety isn't something that has to be overcome once and for all. It's a physiological response to a challenging world. It's the same base instinct that helps us protect ourselves and each other. This story is about harnessing that psychic energy for good and committing to live a life unbound by fear—not a life free of fear. The last few months have reemphasized how vital this point is.

As I pen what is to be the last chapter of this book, I am celebrating Easter, from home, in the midst of a pandemic. Millions of people around the globe are observing this feast, frightened and crippled by the shadow of the novel coronavirus (COVID-19). It is an Easter I could have never imagined.

Churches are locked down across the globe, from Saint Peter's Basilica in Rome to the Church of the Good Shepherd in New Zealand. Even Our Lady of Lourdes Church, which my father revered till his death, is empty. Almost nowhere can believers go to Church this Easter Sunday.

I admit I am observing Easter Sunday, in front of the television, wearing pajamas.

As I write, all 50 states are under federal disaster declarations—a grim first in U.S. history. In New York City, the biggest hotspot for coronavirus in the U.S., Cardinal Timothy Dolan spoke to worshippers online from a virtually empty St. Patrick's Cathedral.

I myself tuned into a homily from Toronto, where Father Michael Coutts spoke about how the uncanniness of our current situation caused him to think of the first Easter Sunday, 2,000 years ago. The apostles were hiding in the upper room with the doors locked because they were frightened of the authorities coming after them. Only one woman, Mary Magdalene, was brave enough to go to Jesus' tomb and find out what had taken place. He praised her bravery in the face of uncertainty.

Two years ago, I was blessed to go to Jerusalem and spend some time at the house where the apostles and the Virgin Mary were hiding in the upper room. I can imagine this brave woman running along the west sector of Jerusalem to the upper chamber to share the message of the resurrection of the Lord with the apostles.

Because of her act of courage, eventually John and Peter traveled to the tomb to corroborate her testimony. When they examined the body wrappings undisturbed with no trace of Jesus, they tentatively believed in a miracle. But what did they truly believe in? What did his resurrection mean?

After all, Lazarus had been resurrected too. The understandably skeptical apostles yearned to see his physical body—to ask questions and to understand. I believe, but I also yearn for answers and understanding. I hope as feebly as they did for the day when the pandemic wanes, and I can hug my loved ones, celebrating Easter in a church like I've been doing more regularly over the past several years.

Like in the days of the early church, these are dangerous moments. From a distance, the apostles had to interpret the signs of the time. They were scared and frightened. Multiple disturbances were going on, and so many people were dying because of their faith. There was uncertainty and doubt in their minds. I had to assume they were also experiencing panic and anxiety, not knowing for sure if Christ had risen. They conditioned their faith to sight and not to an absolute conviction in the scriptural prophecy and the direct teachings by Jesus, proclaiming His resurrection on the third day after His death.

I had always wondered what Jesus felt when he knew he was going to die. What were his anxieties? We all face challenges. The fear of death can cripple and be incapacitating most times. Our first reaction is to cry out to God to spare us. But when we don't receive an answer promptly, we doubt our faith.

The Germans have a characteristically precise word for panic hoarding. The term is *hamsterkauf*, a compound noun made by adding the word "to hoard" with the word "to buy." The word *hasmstern* comes from the name of the animal, the hamster which stores food in its cheeks. We all get anxious and want to save when we think there might be scarcity in the future. It's a biological instinct, experienced even by the little hamster.

The fear is understandable, and in daily life, planning for uncertainty is a good thing. It's why we buy insurance and save for retirement and college funds. But the fear of the future is not unlike what the doubting apostles experienced upon seeing the empty tomb. They had hoped maybe, but they didn't quite believe.

I am not exaggerating when I say that if this current pandemic had occurred when I was in my early 20s, fighting daily anxiety and panic attacks, I might not have survived. The pictures on the television and social media of empty supermarket shelves cleared out of food and other household items such as toilet paper and sanitizers amid the coronavirus outbreak would have sent me into an uncontrollable spin of panic attacks. Over the past several weeks of quarantine, I have relied on coping mechanisms I have learned throughout my life. I stick to my daily routines and rituals, many of which I first learned years ago in psychotherapy.

Reliving parts of my life while writing this memoir has been a trying and a poignant journey. I have had to confront my fears and anxieties one more time. However, it has been a cathartic and liberating experience. Specifically, I had to ask myself if my fear of death, which had crippled me many times, had entirely resolved.

Death seems to be the most common thing around. Every living organism dies. Trees, plants, insects, animals, they all die. We human beings are no exception to the rule. We are part of the natural world, and that world includes death. There are many types of death—psychological, spiritual, physical—which we could all experience.

At the prospect of death, we recoil in horror. I used to tend to look at death as the end, mysterious and unknown. The unknown always terrified me. The image of total darkness away from the source of light still scares me.

Situations, like we are living now, can create anxiety and spur circumstances where people cannot cope effectively. This type of crisis can further exasperate despondency and hopelessness. They can experience the same frustration I experienced when I felt alone with no solution in sight.

That is the reason, as I have learned later in life, to be prepared with a self-care plan which incorporates the mind, the spirit, and our human relationships. In my particular situation, what helped me the most was meditation with a profound reflection on the scripture and Christ.

Those struggling with significant personal and family pain, scary life circumstances, panic attacks, and depression have reported relief through faith-centered daily meditation with astonishing results. We have to forgive and relinquish resentment to those who have offended or wounded us.

Research has shown this approach results in striking physical health, emotional and relationship well-being, easing anxiety and depression while boosting autonomy, self-sufficiency, and relationship stability.

I have tried to focus on the beautiful things I learned from my mistakes and have also discovered internal peace and forgiveness. In reimagining my life, I have come to understand the origin of my fears, anxiety, and panic finally—or at least I think I have.

Maybe most importantly, I'm no longer afraid of dying. Overcoming this fear has been difficult, but I was fortunate to be surrounded by beautiful people who did their best with what they had at the time to protect me and show their love and kindness. They never gave up on me.

As a child, when you experience something traumatic, you almost always think it is your fault. When you depend on your parents, you have minor power to change your circumstances. There are only two options to deal with this matter—either you accept you are powerless or you take universal blame for what is happening to you. Blaming yourself is a protective mechanism to avoid the pain of seeing how vulnerable you were and possibly still are. If it's not your fault, you may not be able to stop it from happening again.

It was later in life, in my early 40s, when I discovered the benefits of exercise in reducing my anxieties and panic. Once I started moving and paying attention to my diet, things changed for me. My outdoor adventures provided me with a much-needed perspective about how my life was minuscule compared to a vast universe of lives—and if my life was small, then my anxieties were even smaller. This awareness helped me shrink down the size of my ego to a manageable size. It was with the help of psychotherapy I could overcome the addiction to the self.

I hope my message is clear and convincing enough to positively alter the lives of others, including my children. I want to express my regrets and shame for having hurt so many dear people in my life, especially my wife. I do not intend to justify my actions, but I want to express my gratitude and love for the people who stuck with me.

Unfortunately, it is too late to apologize to my parents, but I hope they have a copy of my book in heaven and that after reading it, they realize how much I loved them and how regretful I am for not showing them what they meant to me while they were alive.

AFTERWORD

Luis A. "Pochy" Franco, M.D.
Diplomat of the American Board of Psychiatry and Neurology
Associate Professor of Psychiatry
Ponce Health Sciences University
and a friend

ANXIETY IS INHERENT to human nature. Everyone experiences bouts. Clinically, it is defined as a diffuse, unpleasant, vague sense of apprehension where physical symptoms often accompany the psychological.[29]

Anxiety begins the day we are born, and we can't entirely break free of it till the moment we die. It's a biochemical process—neuroanatomical pathways and structures triggered in our amygdala and our locus coeruleus, our hypothalamus, and our raphe nucleus. It's a product of our brains.

Anxiety is not a matter of nature versus nurture. Instead, it is the story of nature and nurture conspiring to condition us.

My friend, Dr. Francisco Torres, asked me to write an afterword to his book, and my first reaction was an almost crippling anxiety. I have been practicing psychiatry for nearly 30 years, and I have always

---

[29] Synopsis of Psychiatry, Kaplan and Sadock's, Benjamin J Sadock , MD and Virginia Alcott Sadock, MD.

wanted to chronicle my own experiences in the field. But writing is a tricky proposition that implicates our ego and our insecurities. I am so proud of Dr. Torres for putting his life down into words so that others—myself included—can benefit from the lessons of his journey with anxiety. So, I am also thrilled to provide some psychiatric context for that story.

First, let me distinguish between fear and anxiety. Both are alerting signals to danger. They both involve the same structures of the brain. But fear is sudden—an acute response to a known, external, definite threat. Anxiety is a slow drip response to an unknown threat—internal, vague, or conflictual.[30]

As Dr. Torres writes in his book, anxiety is not all bad. We need a certain amount. Anxiety inspires us to grow, improve, and to mature. It is responsible for many of the coping mechanisms we develop over the course of our lives. We learn to deal with myriad challenges by mastering our response to the anxieties these challenges provoke.

Still, there is a point at which anxiety becomes pathological. Usually, we diagnose it clinically when the demands from external (relationships, finances, etc.) and internal (separation, rejection, etc.) stressors exceed the capacity of an individual to deal with the symptoms of anxiety, causing us to malfunction or fail to adapt.

Anxiety disorders are among the most prevalent disorders diagnosed by psychiatrists. The National Comorbidity Study reports that one in four individuals suffers from an anxiety disorder. As Dr. Torres' memoir illustrates, these issues can take root early in our lives—sometimes, even before we are born.[31]

Now, let me turn to Kiko. His father showed signs of paranoia and narcissism. His insecurities and catastrophic thinking are typical of genetic pools prone to anxiety and other mental health disorders. Layer onto Kiko's mom, whose acute anxiety ran a straight line from her devastating fear of lightning to a generalized unease with life up

---

30   *Ibid.*
31   *Ibid.*

until the moment of her death. Kiko's genetic background is fertile soil for the blossoming of an anxiety disorder.

But that's not to say we are predestined to any particular mental health disorder. Learning behaviors can also explain anxieties and phobias. As a child, when we experience the adults in our lives reacting to various stimuli with fear, anxiety, or negativity, we can in turn tend to model the same behavior. Kiko's mom may have unconsciously contaminated him with many of these instincts.

One of this book's greatest gifts is the ability it affords us readers to dive into the author's upbringing, and to more fully examine the development of a human psyche. It's something psychologists and literary critics are familiar with, but in our daily lives we interact with each other almost blind to the psychological roots of our behavior.

Kiko's childhood was both normal and calamitous. He is a middle child in a family of three siblings. The memoir describes vacillating idolatry and deep resentment of his older brother—a superstar, intelligent, handsome, the favorite of parents, grandparents, and teachers. Juan Luis gets the validation Kiko so desperately desires. His younger sister benefits from being the baby and the only girl. Without a doubt, we see in this book it was hard for Kiko to get noticed, much less accepted by his family. We also see that he engages in risky, often cruel, behavior in response.

Sibling rivalries are fierce. Sometimes the competition becomes irrational and dangerous. It leaves psychological scars. Kiko's drive to be noticed infected many of his most destructive decisions.

Theories about stress suggest that trauma is cumulative and most impactful the earlier in life we experience it. Structures like the hippocampus—where memories tangle with emotions—can become stunted or malformed by early traumatic experiences. The Freudian and Erikson theories of child development emphasize the significance of early life experiences in the unfurling of psychiatric disorders in adults. Childhood experiences lay the groundwork for our mental health profiles—even the likelihood of developing a condition like post-traumatic stress disorder (PTSD) is affected by childhood stimuli.

My friend Kiko was no stranger to trauma as a child. Drowning is a primordial human fear, and Kiko's first foray into the water branded him with an early phobia. He was inculcated early on with the notion that his birth had been unusually painful for his mother, and his first caregiver—Tia Lola—just disappeared out of nowhere one day. Then Manolito dies. It is devastating enough to have lost a boyhood friend, but to be blamed for the death by your father is poisonous—particularly as you are naturally beginning to deal with concepts like guilt. These experiences weakened Kiko's initiative and self-confidence. Without a doubt, experiences like this contribute to panic and anxiety.

School was no refuge from the tumults at home. The competition with his siblings metastasized into a struggle against bullying seniors and unaccommodating teachers. Kiko's older brother, Juan Luis, charmed the faculty and his classmates. Kiko couldn't live up to the grades or the friends or the affirmations. Mercifully, in middle school, he met a nun who took an interest in him and paved a path to college and a future. Then, he met Elvira—maybe the only, or at least most important, consistent support in his life.

But medical school really renewed the burden of Kiko's anxieties. He was carjacked at gunpoint. In a factual sense, he confronted mortal danger. There begin the first recognizable panic attacks.

Like many who have encountered the disorder, Kiko's panic attacks led to frantic hospital visits. The bubbling of guilt, anxiety, and fear overran his capacity to cope. It led to overpowering feelings of helplessness.

My intention is not to analyze or diagnose Kiko. He is my colleague, my friend, and my *compadre*. I'm his youngest son's godfather. But as a psychiatrist, it's impossible not to consider how several possible mental health circumstances have led him to a place where he can write this book. I believe the trauma of Kiko's carjacking—cushioned on a long developmental history of stress and anxiety—very likely seeded symptoms of post-traumatic stress disorder in his brain.

There are people in the world who characterize mental health disorders and treatments in terms of voodoo science—an obscure excuse for human choices. This couldn't be further from the truth—between our chemistry and our psychology, the challenges we each experience in our lives are different, and while our outcomes are not predetermined, we are predisposed to different things. The good news is that these realities don't mean our mental health disorders are hopeless.

As I've written above, anxiety disorders are exceedingly common. There are excellent treatment options available that boast high success rates. For most of his life, however, Kiko avoided these interventions. How did he come through to the other side?

My hope is that in reading his story you have not focused entirely on the trauma—the parental deficiencies and zany misfortunes. Where our attention must drift is toward the exceptionally positive figures who drove Kiko's progress, and the unwitting coping mechanisms he developed out of necessity. It's a story of hope.

I have identified some of these non-medical interventions throughout the book. Sister Marjolein, for example, who engaged Kiko during a turbulent adolescence, helping him to unravel a competitive edge within himself. She helped him to believe in his drive to succeed, and he responded by getting into college and medical school. To this day, I think the influence is precious for Kiko. Sister Marjolein met an untimely end in Rhodesia on a mission, and one of Kiko's joys is his Rhodesian Ridgeback. It's a special testament to the importance of having characters in our lives who believe in us and who express that belief to us.

The book owes its name to Mr. Winston's prescription to just "keep kicking, Frisco!" Don't think such seemingly small encouragements can't alter the trajectory of a person's life. Some of the most successful people in the world owe their grounding to a personal mantra they can resort to in times of uncertainty. This is Kiko's.

The notion of kicking forward in spite of fear has led Kiko to pilot a Cessna, enter a bodybuilding competition, scuba dive in Tonga and Maui, and run an ultra-marathon at Machu Picchu. Without knowing it, Mr. Winston indoctrinated young Kiko to a type of cognitive-behavioral treatment for anxiety disorders known as flooding.

The psychoanalyst Otto Fenichel described sufferers of phobic anxiety who try to hide behind attitudes and behavior patterns that amount to a denial of the dreaded situation or other stimuli. People who adopt this coping mechanic prefer to confront head-on the catalyst of their anxiety. It's a fascinating rejection of feeling victimized by the disorder.

Flooding is another description of this counterphobic attitude. It is based on the premise that escaping from anxiety-provoking experiences reinforces anxiety through conditioning. Clinicians who practice this kind of behavioral therapy attack the phobia by exposing patients to the provoking situation. Eventually, in many instances, the experience slowly ceases to provoke the same anxious response.

Kiko has done this inadvertently throughout his life, and we can follow his results in this memoir. For example, he addressed his fear of isolation by leaving Puerto Rico for Louisiana, disregarding language barriers, and the lack of contacts on the mainland. His fear of drowning gets treatment on a series of scuba diving excursions. The terror of an untimely death leads him to fly a small airplane. His childhood embarrassment of shirtless beach trips results in bodybuilding competition where he flexes for crowds in speedos. The perennial anxiety he feels over failing health culminates in a sort of spiritual and physical coup de grâce at the finish of one of the world's most challenging ultra-marathons—fittingly amid ancient ruins and primeval beauty.

Despite their failings, Kiko's parents also played a crucially positive role in Kiko's life. They were consistent figures—even if sometimes Kiko might have wished them away. They provided for his education and his growth. Love isn't manifested perfectly in our actions. But you can't read this book and not feel the love that Manoli and Luis had for their son, not to mention his love for them.

It's strange to say of a successful physician, but in many ways,

Kiko is an autodidact. He has spent his life searching for answers to his life's condition. He's no psychologist, but he diagnosed and treated himself pretty ably. His is a powerful story of trial and error. He acted out as a child and realized the burden of that misbehavior was too much to bear—even though there were unquestionable relapses. When he first reached out for professional help, he didn't click with the first therapist, so he moved onto the second, realizing he might do better with a woman. He didn't give up. This led him to Eye Movement Desensitization and Reprocessing (EMDR), which asks a patient to recall distressing memories—at the direction of a therapist—while exposing the patient to stimuli that move the eye from side to side. The idea is to take away the emotional component of the traumatic experience by tethering these memories to harmless somatic movements.[32] It, along with flooding, has worked for Kiko.

I will briefly note here that not everyone succeeds without pharmacological intervention. There is a trove of effective medications we can use to treat anxiety disorders. Kiko's mother, for example, came to rely on benzodiazepine. There are problems with drugs like this—primarily the potential to cause chemical dependency. But new medications address this concern with serotonin reuptake inhibitors, revolutionizing the pharmacological treatment of anxiety disorders, and preventing panic attacks in a way that is compatible with long-term use. Medications are one of the most effective ways to treat anxiety disorders, and that should not go unsaid.

I myself am a psycho-pharmacologist, and I also engage in psychodynamic psychotherapy. I want the reader to understand that seeking professional help for a psychological disorder, like the one Kiko describes, is not a sign of a weakness. It's not a flaw. You don't have to take to the sky in a rickety Cessna or enter body-building competitions to overcome your anxiety. Most of us need help from time to time—Kiko is the first to admit it.

In fact, the beauty of Kiko's story is his admission that we will

---

32   Eye Movement Desensitization and Reprocessing: A Conceptual Framework, Indian J. Psychol. Med. 2010 Jul-Dec: 32(2): 136-140.

not traverse the jungles of life alone. We aren't going to scale the top of the mountain without an Eddie carrying us on his back for a part of the journey. I am so proud he decided to share his life with us.

This book is about hope that life can get better and that there is no single route to happiness and peace. I am confident that Kiko's anxiety disorders are more under control now than they have ever been. But I am also confident that there could be an epilogue to this book written every year on the anniversary of its publication. And in that continued struggle we find the will to improve.

As Benjamin Franklin said, "keep in the sunlight."

MORE BOOKS BY FRANCISCO M. TORRES

Dr. T's Drop The Fat Diet

For years, Dr. T has been helping hundreds of clients achieve body and wellness transformations as incredible as his own. Now you can too with this commonsense, medically tested method to jumpstart your metabolism, plan your meals, and get going toward a new you forever. The results are proven. The plan is simple. All you have to do is dive in.

12 Practical Steps to a New You Forever

Life transformation isn't the stuff of fairy tales. Life transformation is real and it's for you, no matter what your story is or who you may be. Don't let your past define you. Expect progress as you allow us to assist you in planning a practical approach to weight loss, health, and more.

12 Practical Steps to a New You Forever Without Arthritis

This book provides hope to live and, in fact, thrive despite the disease. Here you'll find practical suggestions undergirded by a real passion to help all those who confront the effects of arthritis daily. Because seeing your doctor is not always an option, this book provides a variety of alternative and natural remedies to relieve stiffness and pain.

Provocative Thoughts

These thoughts are living, breathing, and changing every time you read them. Here you'll find a series of questions, vignettes, ideas, frustrations, and observations meant primarily to inspire both action and reflection. Growth has no end and this book is not the destination. Instead, it is the starting point – for me and you.

ABOUT THE AUTHOR

Dr. Francisco Torres was born in Seville, Spain, and gradua- ted Cum Laude from the University of Puerto Rico in 1982 with a degree in Biology. He then attended the Uni- versity of Puerto Rico School of Medicine and was awarded his medical degree in 1986.

He is the author of several books on weight loss, pain management, and health as well as his personal growth book *Provocative Thoughts*.

Most importantly, Dr. Torres is a proud husband and the father of four wonderful children, including Jordi, who authored the foreword to this book.